What Does My Future Hold?

99 ways to plan your life

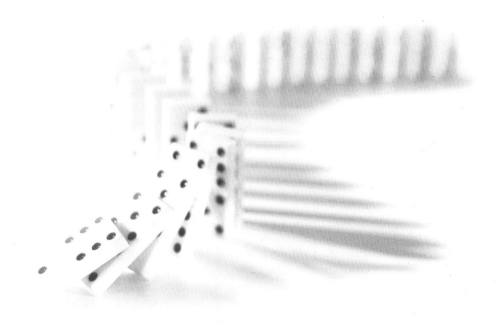

JUDI HALL

PENGUIN COMPASS

PENGUIN BOOKS

Published by the Penguin Group
Penguin Putnam Inc., 375 Hudson Street, New York,
New York 10014, U.S.A.
Penguin Books Ltd, 27 Wrights Lane, London W8 5TZ, England
Penguin Books Australia Ltd, Ringwood, Victoria, Australia
Penguin Books Canada Ltd, 10 Alcorn Avenue, Toronto,
Canada M4V 3B2
Penguin Books (N.Z.) Ltd, 182–190 Wairau Road, Auckland 10,
New Zealand

Penguin Books Ltd, Registered Offices: Harmondsworth,
Middlesex, England

First published in Penguin Compass 2001

1 3 5 7 9 10 8 6 4 2

Created and produced by
CARROLL & BROWN LIMITED
20 Lonsdale Road
London NW6 6RD

Art Editor Tracy Timson
Designer Roland Codd

Text copyright © Judi Hall 2001
Compilation copyright © Carroll & Brown 2001
All rights reserved

ISBN 0-14-019621-8
(CIP data available)

Printed and bound in Italy by Graphicom
Set in Veljovic

ABOUT THE AUTHOR

JUDI HALL has been a karmic counselor for 25 years. Her specialty is past-life reading and regression. She has clients from all walks of life: the House of Lords in the United Kingdom, the European Parliament, pop stars, university professors, scientists, mystics, and people on social security. She has been psychic all her life and has an extensive knowledge of systems of divination.

Judi is the author of many books, including *Deja Who: A New Look at Past Lives*; *Hands Across Time: The Soulmate Enigma*; *The Zodiac Pack: A Visual Approach to Astrology*; *The Hades Moon*; the best-selling *Art of Psychic Protection*; *The Karmic Journey: The Birthchart, Karma and Reincarnation*; *The Illustrated Guide to Astrology*; *The Illustrated Guide to Crystals*; and *Principles of Psychic Protection*.

CONTENTS

Introduction

For I dipt into the future, far as human eye could see
Saw the Vision of the world, and all the wonder that would be
Saw the heavens fill with commerce, argosies of magic sails
Pilots of the purple twilight, dropping down with costly bales
Heard the heavens fill with shouting, and there rain'd a ghastly dew
From the nations airy navies grappling in the central blue

Alfred Lord Tennyson 1808–1892

This book offers you a taste of what the future holds. Based on the most frequently asked divinatory questions, it is a practical, hands-on introduction to the perennially fascinating world of prediction. You will find time-honored methods of looking into the future, plus a unique section on Life Cycles and their unfolding effect on your life. Some techniques have been in continuous use almost since time began. Several oracles have been specially revived for this book, they had their roots in ancient civilizations but were forgotten as the 20th century rushed headlong into the Technological Age. No expensive equipment is required. The oracles are all contained within the book or consist of tools such as coins, playing cards, or dominoes that are found within most homes, or can be improvised if necessary.

The ancients believed that all divination and prophecy came from the gods. For thousands of years, divination was a religious act, the ability granted to a special few. Today, access to divinatory tools is open to anyone. You may ask why you should want to access your future? Isn't this linking into forbidden knowledge? Well, from the beginning of time human beings have been curious about what was to come. Some of the earliest archeological artefacts include scrying mirrors, bones, dice, and other tools for foretelling the future. In some civilizations writing developed so that astronomer-priests could keep track of the stars overhead, and the planetary influence on those below. Seers were highly respected, held in awe for their arcane powers. They guided governments, kings and princes. As an inaccurate prediction could be punishable by death, techniques were constantly refined. To know what the future would bring was to be in control. To create the future by right action was even more powerful.

Man is either a victim of fate or the master of his destiny.

H. Spencer Lewis

This is exactly why people today consult oracles. Whether it is statisticians trying to forecast economic growth, a fashion buyer looking for the next trend, or someone seeking to know the face of his/her future lover — everyone wants to improve his or her fortune by knowing what is to come.

You may query whether it really is possible to look into the future. Will what you see, or what the Oracle tells you, always come to pass? Divinatory tools enable you to explore possibilities for the future, and to access your own intuitive guidance. The future has not yet manifested, so it exists as potential rather than certainty. It is fluid and subject to change. However, enough people through the ages have glimpsed the future to be able to say with certainty that foreseeing what is to come is possible.

Destiny or chance?

Divinatory tools are exactly that: tools. There is no magic involved, no hocus pocus. This is because divination links you to divine guidance through a wise part of yourself that is all-seeing and all-knowing. This wise part is usually hidden from your view, but you can learn to access it and be guided by it in your daily life. It has been the source of visions and inspiration throughout the ages. It is called the intuitive self.

The intuitive self is not limited by time and space. It can move spontaneously into the future, as in dreams and visions. It can gaze into a mirror or candle flame and glimpse what is to come. It can guide the hand that opens a book at exactly the right page for wise guidance. It harnesses the fall of the cards or the coins to spell out the message for us.

Beyond the conscious mind, there are at least two other minds: the subconscious and the collective unconscious. The subconscious mind is your own, but you might not recognize it. It is where intuitions and hunches come from, where forgotten facts lurk, where your deepest motivation is, and where old patterns hold you fast. While your conscious mind might be saying one thing, your subconscious could be creating something entirely different. Oracles can tap into this mind and bring its contents out into the open.

The collective unconscious is more like a group mind. It encompasses everything that has gone before, a sort of psychic web that links all people —

The best way to foresee the future is to create it.

Dr D.G. Rollinson-Gilbert

past, present and future. When oracles tap into the collective unconscious, answers come through archetypes and symbols (something that a time-honored oracle, the I Ching, uses), folk rituals and superstitions. You literally tune into the knowledge of the whole of humankind to find your answers. Like the subconscious mind, the collective unconscious is not limited by time or space — how can it be when it has its roots everywhere? So it can answer questions that take you into the future, or back into the roots of time to receive insight and enlightenment.

Divinatory tools appear to use random chance. Some people believe everything is based on chance, others say there is no such thing. These latter argue that the future is pre-ordained. If an oracle says that something will happen, it is already written. Others prefer to believe that, while the outline of the future may be mapped out, how you deal with the present and what you create for yourself, is up to you. You have freewill and can exercise it.

The view that everything is fate or random chance gives you no control over your life. You feel victim of a malign force or succored by the beneficent whim of fickle fate. The belief that you can align with your destiny by making the right choices, puts you in the driving seat.

Oracles help you to make constructive choices. If, for example, you adhere to the notion that everything is pre-ordained, the name you were given at birth, for instance, sets out your unchanging fate: who you are. But what happens if you change your name? Will your fate remain the same? As we shall see in Chapter One: Your Personal Concerns, this is not necessarily so. The broad outline of what will happen to you may well be mapped out (fate), but your conduct and the choices you make within that framework affect your future. This is freewill in operation. So, if the name you were given at birth is not auspicious, with freewill you are at liberty to change both your name and the future. Indeed, freewill urges you to choose a name that will be auspicious for what you want to do with your life.

Divination and timing

Many questions people ask are "when" questions. "When will I meet my lover?, When will I make my fortune?" Some methods of divination ascertain auspicious moments. By checking your Life Cycles, too, you can see whether you are in an appropriate cycle for an activity. It is pointless starting out on a new venture when in a period of contemplation and withdrawal, just as it is a waste of an opportunity if you do not act decisively at the opportune moment.

The future is fluid and divination has its own peculiar timing. It may also not manifest quite as you pictured it. Oracles are noted for their obscurity. They rarely give straight yes and no answers, and can be misinterpreted according to the preconceptions of the questioner. Things may come out in a roundabout way. An oracle may appear to answer that such and such will happen next week but nothing seems to have occurred — until you apply hindsight. Yes, it happened but not in the way you were expecting. It is always wise to remember that oracles don't do the work for you. You may need to put things in motion yourself rather than sitting back and waiting for things to happen. So a good follow up to "When?" is: "Is there anything I need to do before this can happen?," or "Are there obstacles holding me back?" You also may need to check that you are interpreting the answer correctly — the swing of a pendulum can quickly answer this.

Cause and effect

Much of what seems mystical or magical about foreseeing the future is actually based on cause and effect. Something put into motion at some time in the past has a consequence in the present or future. Oracles simply pinpoint the connection for you. Such connections are obvious when cause and effect occur close together. An example of this is if you are unfaithful to your partner and he or she subsequently leaves you. What may not be so obvious is the insecurity engendered in a person whose partner has a roving eye. Your partner may flirt outrageously at every party but have no intention of taking it further. You, however, may not know this and your own inner doubts and fears are triggered. You may respond by becoming possessive and clinging, or you may flounce off to do your own thing. You could withdraw love, or react with indifference or coldness, and then wonder why your partner prefers the company of someone else. For every unfortunate effect, there has to be a cause. What makes the cause difficult to spot is that so much of it happens below the conscious level — the subconscious mind is at work. This is where divinatory tools help by bringing that cause to your attention. Making appropriate adjustments brings about a new effect.

How to use this book

Across great eons of time and cultural divides, the questions people ask an oracle remain the same. Concerns about the future do not differ. Egyptian pharoahs and commoners who approached *The Egyptian Tablets* had exactly the same challenges as emperors and peasants of dynastic China who called on the *I Ching*, which is why ancient oracles remain so effective today. Those inquirers of long ago share their desire for fore-knowledge with today's seekers after insight. All aspire to know what the future will bring, asking the eternal questions "Where will I find success?," "Will I find love?," "When will I get married?," "What will happen to my children?"

You can use the book to answer specific questions such as these or others dealing with, for example, relationships, work, travel or health, or explore more general questions. But there will be times when you want to know all about an oracle and what it can offer you so that you can apply it to other questions that arise. You will find this information on the oracle feature pages.

There are also questions which are ones of timing that more properly belong to the Life Cycles section rather than to oracles. By familiarizing yourself with this section, you will learn to attune to the inner rhythm of your life and to avoid pushing against your natural flow. "Going with the flow" makes life smoother and more harmonious — but it can equally be fast and exciting as you roll with a cycle of opportunity straight to success.

When the lip is silent,
the heart has a hundred tongues.
Jalal al-din Rumi

Framing your question

To begin, sit quietly with a receptive, open mind while you frame your question. This is not quite as easy as it sounds. It is crucial to word the question correctly and without ambiguity. Asking if it is a good time to buy a lottery ticket might well produce the answer: "Yes," but that does not mean you will win! It may simply be a good time to make a charitable donation or learn a lesson about over-optimistic speculation. If so, there are more direct ways. A better question would be: "If I buy a lottery ticket, will I win?"

When you have your question, identify in what area it falls — **Your Personal Concerns** *(Chapter One)*; **Love and Romance** *(Chapter Two)*; **Family and Home** *(Chapter Three)*; **Education, Money, and Work** *(Chapter Four)* or **Leisure and Health** *(Chapter Five)* and then look at the questions set out in The Contents. These are based on the most frequently asked divinatory questions and you may well find your question here. If it is not, look at the question which is closest and then check to see if your question is also on the relevant page. "Is it over?," for example, also covers "Will s/he come back?," "Should I break off the affair?," and "Is there a chance of reconciliation?" If not, you can adapt questions as appropriate by choosing the one nearest in intent to your own.

Each question is accompanied by one or more oracles that could provide an answer. Some oracles use what appears to be random chance, others are more scientifically based. Where there is a choice, you may feel attracted to only one; if you have a rational approach to life, for example, you may favor a numerical system of looking to the future — or you may wish to try them all. Before you start, take a moment or two to focus on your question. Have it clearly in your mind. Hold the intent that it will be answered in the best, and most clear, way possible.

[An oracle] addresses itself to those thinkers who are compelled by an inner voice to go into the depths of all things, and remains incomprehensible to those who stop at the external meaning of words.

O. Wirth

You can also glance through the book looking to see what catches your eye. As some people are visual, some mind-centered, and others kinesthetic (touch orientated), one approach will feel right for you. You may be touch-orientated and just love the feel of *Dice*, shaking them and rolling them out with tactile pleasure; or you may enjoy handling wood or stone —

in which case **Runes** would be ideal. If you are visual, then **Cards** and **Patterns** appeal. When you are mind-orientated, you enjoy a challenge. **Numerology** or **Astrology** stimulate as well as inform, while **The Hand of Fatima** intrigues everyone.

A symbol can always be studied from an infinite number of points of view and each thinker has the right to discover in the symbol a new meaning corresponding to the logic of his own conceptions.

O. Wirth

Each question generally contains sufficient information right there on the page but in some cases, you may be directed to an oracle feature page or to the Astrological Tables at the back of the book. Some answers may be inconclusive. You may roll the dice but what results may not be one of the answers discussed. Again, you may like to turn to the oracle feature page to determine exactly what your answer means. The feature pages contain all the possible answers. An inconclusive answer could indicate that you should try your question again at a later date — or that you have asked too many questions in one session. However, do bear in mind that what the oracle offers you may be a hint that you are seeking answers in the wrong place, or asking the wrong kind of question. It is so easy to allow preconceptions — or strong desires — to mask the guidance.

"A woman consulted an oracle just before she traveled to England from Australia for a brief visit. Her concern was whether she should leave Australia, which had been her home for twenty-five years, and return to live and work in England. The oracle said that she would meet an old friend who was unhappily married, with whom she would begin a relationship, and that he was the man for her. As the man lived in England, she would return to England. She immediately leaped to the conclusion that this man must be an old boyfriend with whom she had recently made contact again and for whom all the old feelings were there — but who was happily married. In the event, she called in to see a couple she had known for fifteen years and who lived where she was considering making her new home. She found that the couple had just split up and the husband now lived there alone. They struck up an immediate relationship. A few weeks later he went out to Australia to see her. At the end of his visit, this man asked her to return to England to marry him and live in a new house he was building in exactly the place she wanted to live. Had she stuck to her preconception that it was her old boyfriend for whom she was destined, she would have overlooked the real possibility of a fulfilling relationship and the answer to her dilemma."

Once you have mastered the many oracles contained within the book, and you have a particular favorite, it will be possible to use this system to get an answer to your question even where the particular oracle is not given with a similar type of question. Space considerations have meant that not every appropriate oracle can be included each time. In addition to the oracles given under "Should I chance my luck?," **Western Astrology** and **The Square of 36**, for instance, also can pinpoint favorable moments for speculation and expansion — and also indicate when you might be tempted to gamble to excess.

All of us are prophets, not so much from choice as from sheer necessity.
Richard Lewinsohn

Interpreting the answer

Finally a word about the interpretation. Never be afraid to go with your own instinctive feelings about a sign or symbol. Oracles have always been open to personal interpretation — that is part of their mystery. If, when you first see your oracular answer, you instantly think: "Oh, that must mean so-and-so," then you are likely to be right — unless wishful thinking is overcoming intuition. Listening to oracles is all about tuning into your own inner guidance, so be ready to hear it when it speaks to you and do not reject it simply because you do not find that interpretation in this book.

On the other hand, keeping an open mind is essential. If you instantly react with "Oh no, that can't be," then you cut yourself off from the guidance offered

— and from the possibility of change. You may need to develop the question further to clarify matters, or you may simply need to open up your mind to new possibilities.

Oracles may, as already mentioned, give answers that we find ambiguous or unclear. Some answers may be very narrow, others much wider. For example, in "What Career Is Most Suitable For Me?," you may be advised that, as a Leo, your choices would include "solar heating engineer" or "president!" The former is very specific; the latter extremely general — "president of what?" you might ask. The answer being "anything!" This is because Leo is associated with many different things, all giving their own possibilities. It is a fire sign with strong links to the Sun (hence the solar heating) and it also is the sign that has the qualities of regalness and power, with a need to be special (hence the presidential ambitions).

Other oracles have this same combination of specific and general answers, which may lead to confusion. But they could also be pointing to where something else is needed. Consult the **Wheel of Destiny** as to whether you should speculate, for instance, and it might indicate success in a venture, an answer which is fairly wide unless you are asking specifically about a project. It could, however, indicate lucky ventures in commerce which narrows it down somewhat. On the other hand, it might give the specific advice: "Never speculate." Such an answer might not actually be saying "No" to your question. It could be indicating that you need a great deal of preparatory planning, and to ask some very specific questions, before going into the venture. Your common sense and your intuition may be needed to fully understand the answer. If in doubt, listen to your heart rather than your rational mind. This is the place in which the true meaning of an oracle can be heard.

It is not good for all your wishes to be fulfilled:
Through sickness you recognize the value of health,
Through evil the value of good,
Through hunger satisfaction,
Through exertion the value of rest.
Heraclitus

4 9 2
3 5 7
8 1 6

Your Personal Concerns

Perhaps the greatest question of all is "Who am I?" Many people do not really know themselves. They do not know what kind of person they really are, what they are capable of being, nor what would bring them fulfillment in life. Without this fundamental knowledge, life feels flat and tasteless. There is a sense of something missing. The joy of life is lost. The future is bleak. There is no confidence, no self-esteem. And confidence and self-esteem are powerful creators of a good future. If you truly know yourself and your potential, all possibilities are open. The future becomes exciting, challenging, and energizing.

Many of the ancient systems such as astrology — Western and Eastern — Nine Star Ki and Numerology evolved to help you understand yourself and your potential. They are a key to the future.

Your name has always had a powerful magical significance, and, with The Hand of Fatima and Letters of Fortune, if you do not like what it foretells, you can always choose another name and open up a new and more fortunate pathway.

Who am I?

What are my strengths and weaknesses?

What are my talents?

How do others see me?

The name you are known by has great power and significance, as have numbers. The letters of your name can tell you a great deal about your basic character and about the future, and your date of birth has a unique vibration. It is, of course, possible to change your name, but it is impossible to change your birthday. Letters of Fortune offer many insights into your name and others! Your birthdate is used in numerology where it is linked to your Life Number. The vibration of your Life Number is constant. It governs your whole life, a foundation that underpins your evolution. You will always carry the qualities of that number with you, expressing more or less of them at any given time. Your Personality Number, on the other hand, is formed from your full name at birth and is subject to change. Indeed, you can deliberately bring in a new vibration by choosing a new name. The qualities of your Personality Number may be expressed positively or negatively but the potential is always there to use those energies more constructively.

Numerology

This system uses the letters of your name, which can change, and the date of your birth, which does not, to explore your destiny. Your Life Number is created from your birthdate and reveals your basic underlying nature and the qualities you embody. Your Personality Number is derived from your full name at birth and indicates your approach to life and the personality you exhibit. Some numbers — 1 and 5 — are active, outgoing, and positive. Others — 2 and 7 — are receptive, passive, and introspective. If you have a positive approach to life, your numerology will mirror this.

If your Life Number carries very different characteristics from your Personality Number, you may well find yourself confused as to the kind of person you really are. Understanding both numbers helps you to express unexplored parts of yourself, and to capitalize on previously unrecognized talents. On pages 22–25 you will find all you need to know to calculate and interpret your numbers.

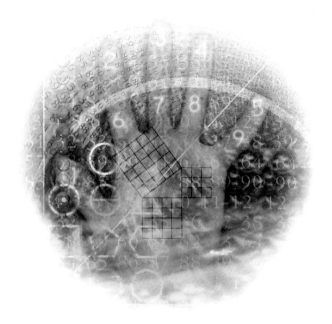

Letters of Fortune

This is another way of looking at yourself through the name by which you are known. Although some of the statements may appear to be contradictory, they can reveal hidden or conflicting aspects that help you to know yourself fully and to maximize your potential. They may also indicate phases of life through which you move and then pass on. If, for example, we look at Judith, Judy, and Judi, we can see how they predict, and affect, a career as a writer.

J indicates intuition, eloquence, and inventiveness—just what a writer needs—while

U warns against exaggeration but points to creative success.

D also indicates success and

I that talent bring rewards.

T shows great imagination—and delight in the weird.

H however warns that literature should be avoided so Judith is not a good name to write under. With Judy, the

Y does not add anything a writer needs so Judi should be adopted instead. To ascertain what your name portends, refer to the pages overleaf.

What's in a Name?

Many people use Letters of Fortune to improve their futures simply by adding or dropping a letter or two and marginally changing the names by which they are known — like spelling Judy with an i as Judi. Or they use Numerology and add an initial or two to their names. These initials do not have to stand for anything; it is the numerical value of the letter that is significant. If you, having added up the number of your name, find it does not resonate with your purpose in life, or fails to bring you good fortune, then you can add initials to change that vibration.

You should have any new spelling, or expanded version of your name, printed on checks, business cards, letterheads, etc. to ensure that good fortune follows.

The two oracles also can be used to find a totally new name if you want release from a family or ex-husband's name or if you are looking for a "professional" name. Check the numerical value of the name before adopting it, and make any adjustments to spelling to improve the numerical value. (Numerically speaking, Robins is more auspicious than Robbins for someone seeking to make a mark on the world. Robins is a 5 — active, outgoing, and resourceful. Robbins is a 7 — reflective, passive, and introspective).

Letters of Fortune

*The origins of this ancient system of divination are lost
in time. All you need to do is check the meanings beside
each letter of your first name. Letters of Fortune is based
on the name by which you are most often known, and
as this may well differ from your birth name, it can be
instructive to look at both your birth name and the one
by which you are now known, so that you can see areas
of your life which have fallen away and others which
come into prominence with the change of name.
Letters of Fortune also shows you what is waiting in the
future, and how to make changes in your fortunes.*

Method

Use the name by which you are most often known. It is
usual to use only one name but if you have a
professional name that consists of a personal name and
surname, for instance, you might want to see the
different influences this brings into your life.

Look up interpretations for each letter separately.

Make a note of them.

Be honest with yourself. Do these statements reflect the
true state of affairs? Check with a friend or your partner
— if you dare.

Having consulted Letters of Fortune, you might like to
see if changing the spelling of your name will bring in
a different, preferable vibration. You can also choose
letters that bring in an appropriate possibility and
arrange them into a new name. You may also find that
your given name at birth reflects aspirations your
parents had for you rather than what you truly wish for
yourself. In which case, choose a new name!

A

Vitality and enthusiasm
inspire others.
Prone to ill health,
common sense overcomes.
Irritability and "nerves"
create financial and
domestic problems.
Engaging in new activities
overcomes shyness.
Unforeseen events may
cause unexpected move to
faraway place.
Travel widely, may choose
to live far from home.
You could well suffer
through own fickleness.
Ambition attained through
application and skill.

B

Lack ability to manage
people with thoughtfulness
and honesty.
Naturally adaptable,
handle any problem
provided extremes are
avoided.
Think before you act, pay
attention to detail or plans
will be defeated.
Be actively engaged in
projects to be happy.
Generosity may interfere
with artistic talent.
Curtail stubbornness or
become discouraged.

C

Excellent understanding of
people.
Avoid lengthy discussions
as these undermine.
Unwilling to attend to small
problems and details, but
common sense overcomes.
Intelligence shines brightly,
propelling into positions of
importance.
Modify impulsive
tendencies by analyzing
situations first.

D

Excellent judgment, you
weigh things carefully. Do
not be discouraged, success
lies ahead.
Brusqueness and
forcefulness are your
undoing.
Overcome inferiority
complex, patient efforts
will be rewarded.
Afraid of nothing,
nevertheless stay out of
physical fights.

E

Timidity recedes as you mature.

Secretiveness and selfishness give power, lose support unless craving for money and power moderated.

Innate intelligence and diplomacy bring ambition to fruition.

Versatility brings honors, do not become careless.

Use, develop, and apply imagination and succeed, but avoid irrationality.

If you knew what people really think of you, you would be surprised.

F

Overwhelming pride, beware of a fall.

Do not put trust in superstitions.

Desire for justice brings enduring friendships.

Works well under direction, natural team player.

Avoid conceit, especially over artistic abilities.

Pursued diligently, talent and intelligence take you far.

G

Your morbidity disturbs those around you.

Enjoy needed solitude, outdoor activities are beneficial.

Indifference hurts yourself most of all.

Base activities on realism.

Care with money attains desire.

Excesses are harmful.

Reason carries you through roughest times.

H

Happiness comes from pursuing ideal.

Music and art enhance achievements, ignore literature and drama.

Criticism hurts.

Numerous talents, concentrate on one to find fame.

Status not enhanced by bragging.

I

Efforts rewarded by beautiful family life.

Opposite sex can be a nuisance.

Talent is your greatest love and inspiration.

Inconstancy causes great anguish.

Empathy and human understanding bring rewards.

Cleverness may interfere with physical desires.

Do not confuse sensuality with love of family.

Follow your ideals.

J

Intuition is useful, rely on it.

Eloquence expresses gifted mind.

Business schemes are dangerous, beware.

Inventiveness, well-managed, brings wealth and high position.

Channel energy into helping others.

K

Love of home increases security.

Strong desire for independence should not be taken to extremes.

Control lust for power as it may overwhelm.

Instincts of a good director, meddling can weaken position.

Discretion and moderation important factors in life.

L

Sobriety and thoughtfulness promote talent.

Secrets of magic and mystery are yours if you desire.

Control sexual urge to avoid unpleasant situations and relationships.

Avoid the supernatural, it has nothing to offer.

To achieve success and happiness, first overcome hatred and jealousy.

Spiritual studies beneficial.

Outdoor occupations make money.

M

Physical comfort and wealth matter most.

Over-indulgence and bad habits are your undoing.

Respect for religion brings peace of mind.

Avoid risks, they destroy stability.

Keep finances under control or they create mental stress.
Avoid morbidness to find success.

N

Indecision worst enemy, only you can overcome.
Overcome innate fears by self-development and latent talent.
Impulsive nature could get you into serious trouble.
Overcome tendency to unpredictability and irritability, then many friends and prosperity.
Imaginary problems could overwhelm, stay in the here and now.

O

Constancy and truth as friend or lover earns great happiness.
Ruled by head not heart, search far and wide for your path.
Selfishness will defeat plans unless you modify demands.
Sedentary habits are bad for you, keep active.
Misfortune the consequence of own recklessness.
Fantasy and illusions mar love life.
Devotion will be rewarded.
Flirtatious habits lead to disappointment and bad luck.
Idealist in love, take time choosing mate.

P

Follow artistic ability to brilliant career.
Practical ability can bring great financial reward.
Attractiveness demands plenty of common sense.
Literature, music, and art bring what you most desire.
Great future if you concentrate on most obvious talent.

Q

Actions should be determined by science and reason.
Cleverness takes you far in business or industry.
Get an agent to promote your ideas.
Love for humanity places in the right profession.
Risky schemes may bring serious trouble.
Look for the best in everything, but avoid over-optimism.

R

Powers of persuasion bring a position of prominence.
Evasive nature sooner or later marks you as schemer.
You will make money in business.
Make career one of the professions.
Scheming mind and oratory do well in politics.
Invent something, make it practical.
Expend too much energy on too many projects, fail.
Adventurous spirit brings changes.

S

Talent is great, but do not overrate.
Pursue greatest talent and luck is at your side.
Gifted, you bring gaiety into lives of others.
Enchanting personality, help others toward prosperity as well as yourself.
Fearlessness and versatility bring spectacular career, provide for old age.
Do not dream about unrealistic goals, be practical and carve out a career.
Great vision, do not overlook what is already attained.
Originality, do not scatter energy or talent unwisely.
Articulate, disorganized and mean, seek advice in all transactions.

T

Great imagination your finest talent. Use appropriately to enjoy riches and honor.
Restless, nervous and petulant, seeking companionship.
Change of surroundings often helps.
Fantasy and delight in the weird assist in new endeavors.

Study a factual subject, especially history.
Impulsive with low boredom threshold.
Intensive study satisfies not, metaphysical interests do.
Good imitator, needing enterprising people around.

U

Take great pride in achievements, which are noteworthy.
Family and home are pride and joy, give them attention.
Boasting about success ends in disappointment.
Avoid vulgarity, it has no place in your life.
Lack of respect may hamper. Boost another and see how life changes.
Altruism brings unexpected happiness and financial reward.
Adhere to ideals, they bring recognition.
Beware of egotism, it could be your downfall.
Honesty brings honor and distinction.
Intolerance and fanaticism could ruin you.
Versatility and creativity find a place in exalted undertakings.
Avoid exaggeration, adhere to the truth.
Remain practical to bring stability in family, business, and social life.
A perfectionist, taken to extremes: impossible.

V

Unorthodox views, often correct, keep them to yourself.
Affinity with land could bring prosperity through real estate.
Music and poetry express introspective, melancholy nature.
Apply mathematical ability to another science, despite doubt.
Overcome unsociability, lead a happy life.
Practical rather than studious, a good job.
Avoid metaphysics, adhere to family values.

W

Put aside indolent ways, talent brings money you so enjoy.
Keen mind, make fortune in business.
Excellent business ability needs to be kept on track.
Avoid impulsiveness, but give free rein to originality.
Use sympathetic nature in caring profession or service.
Inherent love of science, capacity for innovative research.

X

Wonderful talent accompanied by common sense.
Combine merchandising with artistic abilities for success and fulfillment.
Engineering good profession until niche found for artistic skills.
Write as a hobby until it has proved its worth.
Take head out of the clouds, apply yourself, fantastic career.
Love of publicity and excitement, enjoy public appearances.

Y

Channel aggressiveness into selling to find success.
A fighter, apply to achieving desires.
Courage to stand by decisions no matter what opposition.
Do not look for trouble.
Quarrels will not solve anything.
Seek advice before you get into a difficult situation.
Attracted to military, may be hard to choose between home and country.

Z

An idealist, but calculating.
How far to go? Only you can decide.
Pride does not allow concessions.
Ability to appraise situations accurately brings success.
Respect for others minimal, you know your ability outshines them.
Apply vanity to home and surroundings, so no harm comes of it.
Avoid boasting, do the unexpected, keep ideals, and attain goals.

Numerology

Numbers can map out your destiny and your potential, your personality, and your inner self. This method of prognostication goes back to ancient Chaldea, and the Hebrew Kabbalah that developed from it, and to the visionary Greek mathematician Pythagoras who taught that number was the essence of all things, reflecting the order hidden behind the apparently random nature of the universe. Pythagoras believed that number was a key that unlocked the secrets of the psyche and the soul. His mystery school had an enormous influence on Greek thinkers such as Plato and Aristotle, and, via the Italian Renaissance, on modern civilization.

Nowadays there are several systems of numerology, each differing slightly from one another, but the basic precept remains the same: each number has a unique resonance and all numbers reveal a purposeful, unfolding pattern.

$$7 + 8 + 5 + 3 + 9 = 32 = 3 + 2$$

1	2	3	4	5	6	7	8	9
A	B	C	D	E	F	G	H	I
J	K	L	M	N	O	P	Q	R
S	T	U	V	W	X	Y	Z	

Life Number

Your birthdate produces your most basic and fundamental number, your Life Number, which is fixed and unchanging. A dominating influence throughout your life, it indicates your life purpose and lessons you have to learn. Your Life Number represents special characteristics and attributes that may be modified slightly by unfolding cycles but which will always form part of your inner being.

Method

Add together the individual digits of your birthdate, including your birth year in full, until reduced to a single digit. (Note, however, that 11 and 22 are master numbers that have their own interpretation.)

Example If you were born on November 25 1943, your Life Number would be 8

$$1 \mid 1 \mid 2 \mid 5 \mid 1 \mid 9 \mid 4 \mid 3 = 26 = 2 + 6 = 8$$

The Numbers

1 Bold, dominant, powerful, pioneering, imaginative.

2 Passive, receptive, intuitive, harmonizing, emotional.

3 Creative, active, versatile, independent, idealistic.

4 Logical, practical, reliable, down-to-earth.

5 Active, freedom-loving, resourceful, curious.

6 Nurturing, concerned, creative, idealistic, caring.

7 Reflective, observant, analytic, inventive, contemplative.

8 Authoritative, energetic, responsible, persevering, spiritual.

9 Compassionate, impersonal, creative, dramatic, impressionable.

Personality Number

This shows how you approach life and how you handle challenges, and sets out your basic personality and the face you present to the world. Your "outer personality" is shown by the numerical value of the consonants in your name. Your "inner self," which may be very different, is represented by the vowels. Added together, vowels and consonants produce the integrated Personality Number.

Having different layers of number helps you to understand yourself deeply. If your outer personality has a number that is the same as, or harmonious with, your inner person, self-expression is uncomplicated. Where your outer personality and your inner self have inharmonious numbers, the result can be conflict. The face you show to the world may mask a very different set of inner needs, which have been denied expression.

Method

Referring to the table of Numerical Values, calculate the value of the consonants and vowels in your name, and then calculate the value of the total name.

Example	P	Y	T	H	A	G	O	R	A	S	
Vowels					A		O		A		
					1		6		1		= 8
Consonants	P	Y	T	H		G		R		S	
	7	7	2	8		7		9		1	= 41 = 4+1 = 5

Personality Number 8 + 5 = 13 = 1 + 3 = 4

You then need to refer to the Personal Numbers Chart overleaf to see the characteristics of each number and to interpret harmonies and clashes. Besides referring to inner and outer expression of basic energies, life purpose, and character traits, numbers may have a free flow of energy or a blocked flow. If the flow is blocked, the number is experienced negatively. If it flows freely, it is constructive and positive. To fully understand Pythagoras, read numbers 8, 5, and 4 to see how they differ and where they are in harmony. We can identify his need to integrate material success with spiritual insights (8) and to balance freedom and discipline (5) which was expressed through his School. We also can see how his number system brought form into matter (4). His need to be in control (8) would no doubt have made him a demanding teacher but one who could deal well with people (5) although his personality may have been rigid (4).

Personality Numbers

1 The Self and the reasoning mind Energetic, confident, creative, outgoing. Natural leader with strong will. Likes to be in control. May dominate.
Blocked expression Addiction, frustration, insecurity, willfulness, egotism, intolerance.

2 The spirit of cooperation and harmony Supportive, caring, sensitive, efficient. Looks for security and stability. Passive and receptive. Helper.
Blocked expression Over-critical, indecisive, over-adapting, overly servile, helps then suddenly withdraws.

3 The urge for emotional expression and sensitivity Sensitive, active, sociable, articulate. Successful. Inspired. Idealistic, the eternal optimist.
Blocked expression Fear of rejection, attention seeking, conceit, deceit, depression, over-sensitivity.

4 The number of form and matter Logical, secure, reliable, dependable. Calmly efficient, makes patient progress. May be too reserved; needs to be flexible.
Blocked expression Impatient, impractical, unstable, fixed in ways.

5 The balance between freedom and discipline Freedom-loving, energetic, spontaneous, restless. Multifaceted. Lively, witty mind. Sociable. Versatile communicator, deals well with people.
Blocked expression Scattered, irresponsible, over-cautious, unreliable.

6 The number of love Comforting, diplomatic, accepting. Giving and caring. Seeks balance and harmony Excellent in business and handling money.
Blocked expression Perfectionism, self-indulgence, selfishness, possessiveness, jealousy.

7 The need to develop trust Meditative, introverted, aloof. Journeying inward, dreams of a better world. Discriminating, analytical, and observant.
Blocked expression Suspicion, escapism, bitterness, betrayal, lack of trust.

8 The need to integrate material success and spiritual attainment Generous, determined, trustworthy. Good organizer suited to responsibility, but may appear demanding as likes control.
Blocked expression Sabotages self, slave-driver, obsessive about money.

9 The number of completion Dynamic, charismatic, independent. Evolved soul but still has lessons to learn. Needs self-control and self-understanding.
Blocked expression Selfish, dissipates talents, bigot.

11 On a mission Powerful leader and formidable enemy. Impressive powers of persuasion.

22 Special person Strong and masterful. Enormous potential if handled well.

Fadic Numbers

Your Fadic Number takes you even deeper into understanding yourself. It is found by adding your Life and Personality Numbers until you have a single digit. It is the number of fate or destiny, which many people see as a karmic number, offering an insight into your life lesson and life purpose.

1 Changing fortunes early in life followed by stability and realization of ultimate aim. Position of prominence and influence, looked to by others for guidance. Organizational skills brings prosperity.
Lesson and purpose Guiding others wisely.

2 Suited to jobs with people contact, especially in partnership with others. Emotional rather than logical response to situations can lead to being duped by others.
Lesson and purpose Developing discrimination and appropriate level of trust.

3 Full of enthusiasm, may go overboard. An above average number of opportunities in life eventually offers substantial gains.
Lesson and purpose Developing common sense to balance natural optimism.

4 Independent, revels in a life of challenge and uncertainty, meeting each head on. Highly resourceful, but often lacks self-control.
Lesson and purpose To temper courage with self-discipline.

5 A restless disposition. Travel looms large in this life. Good at initiating but not at carrying things through.
Lesson and purpose To develop staying power.

6 Adaptable and accommodating, seeking harmony in all things. Easily find friends. Tendency to submerge own needs.
Lesson and purpose To serve others without giving away one's own self.

7 Ability to grasp opportunities and turn them to own advantage. Tendency not to plan leads to disconnected incidents rather than steady progress.
Lesson and purpose To develop clearly defined goals that support life purpose.

8 Ability to make slow and steady progress. Highly industrious and determined to overcome obstacles.
Lesson and purpose Taking advantage of natural persistence to reach aims without becoming mired down.

9 Initiative and the enterprise to make bold moves in moments of crisis despite opposition from others. Prone to unnecessary risks so fortunes fluctuate.
Lesson and purpose To use initiative wisely for reliable growth.

11 The master number of creative energy, holding the promise of worldly success.
Lesson and purpose To utilize the creative force for the good of oneself and others.

22 The master number of perfection. An idealist with humanitarian instincts.
Lesson and purpose To strive for a cause without thought of reward for self.

Why am I here?

What am I meant to be doing
with my life?
What is my spiritual pathway?
How can I find inner fulfillment?

*Many systems of divination have the belief that there is
a "life path" or life purpose which has to be followed if
you are truly to fulfill your destiny. The life path is the
path of the soul, the divine part of a person. Such a
belief frequently arises from the spiritual or religious
foundation of the oracle concerned. In Indian thought,
karma is the path that you follow because it is what you
earned in other lives, but dharma is your life purpose.
When you live out your dharma, you are aligned with
your soul's purpose. Runes can give you a quick
indication of your life's pathway.*

Runes

Meaning "mystery" or "secret" these enigmatic letters
have particular meanings and can be read at many
levels. The interpretations given here relate specifically
to finding your life purpose and spiritual pathway. See
pages 166–9 for how to make your own runes and for a
more general understanding of them.

Select one rune only from your rune bag and read its
meaning. If the rune is reversed (upside down) this
indicates that you will have to search harder for your
pathway, or make adjustments in your life. You may
need to make sacrifices to follow your path.

Mannaz Right
relationship with
one's Self.
Finding the
divine within.

Gebo Finding
true and equal
partnership.
Retaining
separateness in
unity.

Ansuz
Developing the
intuition.
Communication
on all levels.

The blank rune
The path of total
trust.

Othila Path of
submission and
renunciation.
Separation from
past.

Uruz Self-
change through
endings and new
beginnings.
Service.

Perth Deep and
difficult trans-
formation, and
letting go. Inner
reflection.

Nauthiz Identifying and owning the shadow. Reparation and rectification.

Inguz Freedom from the past. Centering and grounding.

Eihwaz The path of patience and perseverance. Overcoming obstacles.

Algiz Control of the emotions without disconnection.

Febu Mindfulness and awareness. Nourish oneself and others.

Wunjo The path of understanding. Alignment of self to Self.

Jera Going with the flow. Attuning to natural cycles.

Kano The rune of opening. Altruism, non-attached giving.

Teiwaz The path of discrimination, courage, and dedication.

Berkana The cycle of growth and self-becoming.

Ehwaz The path of move-ment. Slow and steady progress.

Laguz Being. Experience life without analysis or evaluation.

Hagalaz The Great Awakener. "Radical discontinuity". Using inner strength.

Raido Aligning to divine will. Right action.

Thurisaz Contemplation and non-action.

Dagaz Total transformation.

Isa Surrender and sacrifice of the ego.

Sowelu The path of wholeness. Self-realization with Love.

What will my future be?

Where does my happiness lie?

Having found out who they are and why they are here, the next question people ask is: "What is going to happen to me?" They often have a sense that things are mapped out, or fated, and can be quite surprised when it is suggested that their futures are fluid. They are even more surprised when it is suggested that they create the future. In all systems of divination, opportunities unfold from moment to moment. If those opportunities are grasped, one future emerges. If they are ignored, another future takes over. Playing Cards offer a quick method of determining where you'll find happiness; The Hand of Fatima can enable you to know what your future might be.

Playing Cards

An ordinary pack of playing cards can show in which area of life you will find your greatest happiness.

Method

- Using a full pack of cards, shuffle them well.
- Cut the cards and deal the top five cards, face down, in front of you.

- Turn the cards over and count the number of cards of each suit.
- If you have an equal number of cards from different suits, the higher value cards are the strongest (note that an Ace is 1, a Jack 11, Queen 12, and King 13).

Diamonds Your greatest fulfillment in life comes from nurturing and serving others.

Hearts You will find your happiness arises from friendships and social contacts.

Spades Your deepest contentment comes from traveling the world and opening to new cultures and experiences.

Clubs Your satisfaction comes from making money and the business interests you develop.

The Hand of Fatima

Using The Hand of Fatima (see overleaf), you can pinpoint your own strengths and weaknesses, and gain an indication of what the future has in store.

Your name computes into one or more numbers, which are shown on the hand, and they relate to different parts of your life. As your Individual Number usually has to be broken into component parts, they can show different periods in your life. For instance, if you have 800 and 46 and are at present living in a city and striving for financial success, 800 indicates success and exile, while 46 suggests abundance and life in the country. So, you could well find yourself in a much better financial position and able to move from the city to the country. This could, however, initially feel like being exiled.

You also can use The Hand of Fatima to see if you will be victorious in any kind of competitive situation — personal or business.

Happiness or Fulfillment?

Many people seek happiness. A happiness that consists of getting all their needs met, every desire satisfied. They believe that if they can find the right partners and jobs, all the money they crave, the perfect place to live, and so on, then they will be happy. However, when such "happiness" has been achieved, life can still feel empty. There may well be a deeper purpose to life than mere happiness. So a better question to ask is "What will fulfill me?" or "In which area of life will I find the greatest satisfaction?" Such fulfillment may entail giving up some of the things that, on the surface, brought happiness. So often the seemingly catastrophic events such as loss of job, health, or partner, actually offer the opportunity to move into a deeper fulfillment in life — which is why looking to the future does not always reveal roses all the way. In Chinese, the same character is used for "crisis" and "opportunity." This wise race recognized the connection between the changes that fate appears to inflict on an apparently happy person, and the inner need for fulfillment. The "crisis" brings the opportunity for change. Fortunately, happiness and fulfillment can coincide if you seek both in an appropriate part of life.

The Hand of Fatima

This is said to show your temperament, character, and abilities based on the numerical value (the Individual Number) of the name by which you are known. To find out your basic temperament, consult the Table of Individual Numbers. As you can use this system to look up the numbers of partners, friends, employers or children, you may like to consult this table before you name a child or if you intend to select a new name for yourself. This can be especially helpful when adopting a new professional or pen name, as you can bring in the vibrations you require for good fortune.

The Hand can indicate areas where happiness will be found and weaknesses have to be overcome. Career potential can also be highlighted, as may future possibilities. If you are seeking to overcome a rival, then the Table of Victories will help you.

Method

Write down your personal name and surname, spacing the letters well apart.

Take each word in turn and place below each letter the appropriate numerical values taken from the Upper Hand.

Add up the values for each name, and then add them together. This is the Individual Number.

Consult the Table of Numerical Correspondences.

If the whole number is not shown, split the Individual Number into component numbers and combine the individual correspondences to create the reading. For example, my name.

Example

J	u	d	y	H	a	l	l	
600	200	4	400	8	1	20	20	= 1253

I would look at numbers 1000, 200, 50 and 3 on the Table of Numerical Correspondences.

This would categorize me as someone whose ambition was fulfilled but who is indecisive, into mysticism, fantasy, and spiritual love. After a period of restriction, liberty would bring happiness.

Apparent incongruities may relate to different stages of life or to conflicting parts of the personality. Such conflicts can explain a great deal if you view them with an open mind.

Table of Numerical Correspondences

1 Passion, ambition, drive.

2 Endings, crisis, new beginnings.

3 Mysticism, fantasy, spiritual love.

4 Daring, wisdom, power.

5 Happiness, wealth, marriage.

6 Perfectionism, work.

7 Meditation, pure feelings.

8 Love of justice, honesty.

9 A difficult time with problems.

10 Fulfillment, righteousness, future happiness.

11 Failings, difficult success.

12 Good fortune, success.

13 Cynicism.

14 Devotion, altruism.

15 Cult of the beautiful and ideal.

16 Bliss, voluptuousness, love.

17 Flighty inconstancy.

18 Incorrigible obstinacy.

20 Sadness, sternness.

21 Aggression, violence.

22 Invention, prudence, mystery.

24 Indifference, egoism.

25 Intelligence, fertility.

26 Likes to be useful.

27 Courage and firmness.

28 Tenderness and love.

30 Marriage, fame.

31 Ambition and glory.

32 Celibate, chaste.

33 Exemplary behavior.

34 Suffering and tribulations.

35 Physical and mental health.

36 Genius, prodigious ideas.

37 Virtuous, long-standing relationship.

38 Acquisitive, envious.

40 Celebration, pleasure.

41 Lacking self-worth.

42 Journeys, challenges.

43 Spiritual teacher, ritual.

44 Power, pomp, honor.

45 Creative, many children.

46 Abundance, country life.

47 Carefree life, longevity.

48 Legal matters, judgment.

50 Restriction, then liberty, happiness.

60 Outlives partner.

70 Love of science.

73 Enjoys nature and simplicity.

75 Sensitivity, affection, philanthropy.

77 Repentance, forgiveness.

80 Illness, cure, long life.

81 Artistic, intellectual.

90 Lack of foresight.

100 Honor and glory.

120 Loyal, patriotic.

150 Flattery, hypocrisy.

200 Indecisiveness.

215 Accident prone.

300 Philosophical mind.

313 Intuition, clarity.

350 Naivety.

360 Sociable, many talents.

365 Calculating, self-interest; egoism.

400 Art, love, quick tempered.

490 Secretiveness, mysterious, fervent.

500 Election, honor, fame.

600 Victim of envy, success, and reversal of fortune.

666 Underhand plotting, loss of status.

700 Strength, vigor, health.

800 Success, exile.

900 Bravery rewarded.

1000 Ambition fulfilled.

1095 Victim mentality.

1260 Tribulations, happy old age.

1390 Physical weakness, mental strength.

Victory or defeat?

The Hand of Fatima is also said to indicate who will be victorious in a competitive situation, such as overcoming a rival in love or a business adversary. Using the Wheel below the Hand, compute the value of each personal name and divide it by 9. The remainder number is the Victory Number.

Consult the Table of Numerical Victories to see which name will triumph or whether the two are equally balanced — in which case, the outcome is still undecided and you may need to consult another oracle to see what will give you an advantage over your rival.

Example

$$Judy = 20 + 2 + 24 + 6 = 52$$

divide $9 = 5$ remainder 7

Victory Number 7 beats names totaling 2 and 4, but is overcome by 1, 3, and 5. The numbers 6 and 8 are ambiguous but favor the person asking the question.

Changing your name to change the future

You may also like to compute the number for other names by which you are known such as a diminutive of your personal name; a pen or professional name; a nickname or spiritual name. For women, it is possible to ascertain how a change of name on marriage affects you. If you have been given a spiritual name by a guru or teacher, great insight can be obtained by calculating the different numerical value to that of your birth name.

Table of Numerical Victories

1 overcomes	2	3	7	9
2 overcomes	1	4	6	8
3 overcomes	2	5	7	9
4 overcomes	1	3	6	8
5 overcomes	2	4	7	9
6 overcomes	1	3	5	7
7 overcomes	2	4	6	8
8 overcomes	1	3	5	7
9 overcomes	2	4	6	8

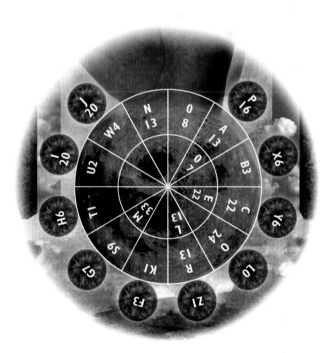

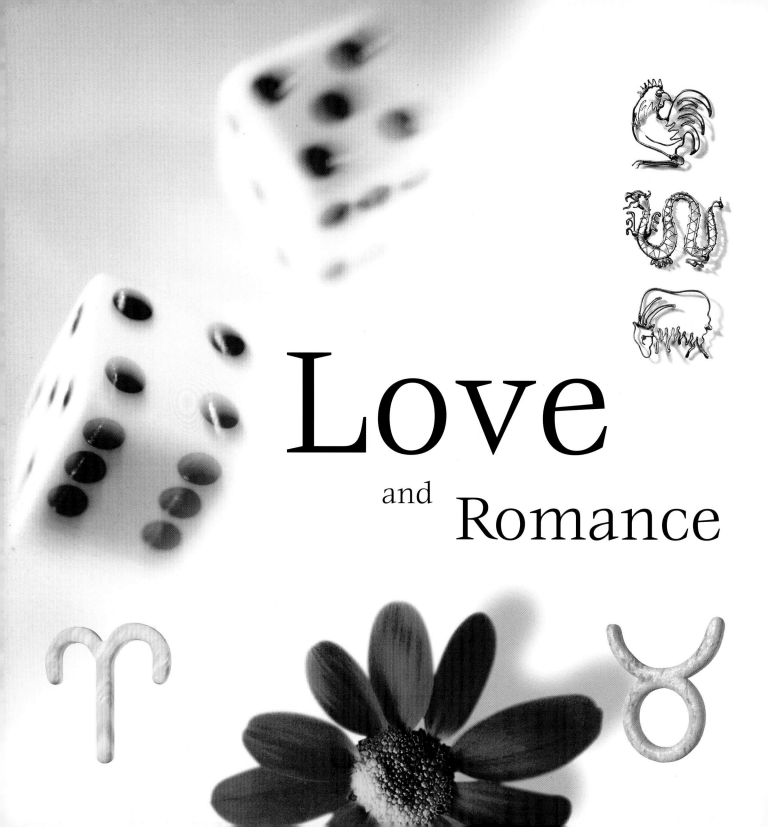

Love
and Romance

M ost people seek a soulmate: the one and only person who can make them feel whole, loved, and totally supported. With this person they believe life will miraculously change for the better. Some people are fortunate enough to find their "other half" and then cease consulting oracles.

Love, however, did not always determine a union. In some cultures, suitability of a mate was indicated through astrology and auguries, and these are still useful tools for determining compatibility. Moreover, having found a partner, enquiries could be made for future happiness and an auspicious day for the wedding. In China and India, no one would choose a wedding day without an astrologer or I Ching master. Nowadays an auspicious day is still important.

Enquiries on matters of love may continue even when a partner is found. Before, and after, marriage, other concerns arise. Insecurities in love are common. "Why, having found my soulmate, am I so unhappy?" The soulmate has someone else, has personal problems or is ill, does not see the other half, or has left. Problems occur because people believe that there is only one soulmate — but there can be more — and that a soulmate is here to make you happy. This, too, isn't true.

"Is s/he faithful?" is a frequent inquiry. Methods of divination arose which focused on these matters. Palmists recognize the flirt, philanderer, two-timer — and the couple headed for divorce. You can use their insights to allay, or confirm, your own fears.

A modern concern is how to end a relationship. Is divorce appropriate? Will the children suffer? Used wisely, oracles guide you through disentangling your life from another. Bear in mind that there is an enigmatic nature to oracular replies. Things may not be what they seem.

Am I going to meet a lover soon?

Will I get a date?

Should I start looking for romance now?

Is this a good time to look for a partner?

Finding a mate is an abiding quest and a subject on which oracles of all kinds can be consulted. Unfolding Life Cycles (see page 177) can indicate if the time is right for meeting a lover. If it is, it will happen; if it is not, nothing will occur.

There are times when you can prepare for this momentous event. But there also are periods that suit introspection, change, and waiting for new possibilities to emerge. So, attuning to the natural cycles of life brings you right timing. For guidance, you can look to the stars; the amorous planet Venus is a classical indicator of love. She makes a yearly journey around your birthchart. If you consult an astrologer about your love life, he or she will invariably look to where Venus resides. A likely moment for romance is when this planet sashays through the part of your chart concerned with love affairs. A more lasting love may be found as Venus moves through your House of Marriage.

Runes, Dominoes, Love Dots, and Cards, these, too, can indicate a fortunate time for love.

Western Astrology

If you know your birthchart, look at the Fifth or Seventh House. If not, counting your Sun sign as number 1, count four more counterclockwise to the fifth sign to find your House of Love Affairs. Go to the seventh sign to find your House of Marriage. Consult the Astrological Tables (see pages 185–8) to find when these points are being activated by Venus to attract love and romance into your life.

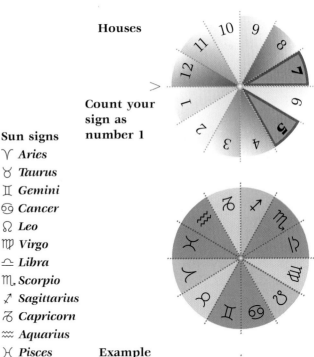

Houses

Count your sign as number 1

Sun signs

♈ *Aries*
♉ *Taurus*
♊ *Gemini*
♋ *Cancer*
♌ *Leo*
♍ *Virgo*
♎ *Libra*
♏ *Scorpio*
♐ *Sagittarius*
♑ *Capricorn*
♒ *Aquarius*
♓ *Pisces*

Example

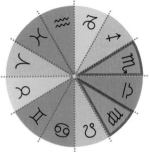

Jane is a Taurean. Her Fifth house is Virgo and her Seventh is Scorpio. Venus moves through these houses in the fall and early winter. This is her best time for romance.

Playing Cards

A deck of cards can tell you when love and marriage will arrive in your life. They also can warn you of any unfortunate consequences, stumbling blocks or delays.

Method

Shuffle a full pack of playing cards several times. Cut the cards and put the pack together again. Lay out the cards face up in nine horizontal rows as shown. Begin with the top row of nine cards, laying them down from right to left. Lay each row beneath, starting one card in. You will have seven cards left over; place these face up away from the triangle.

If card number 9 in the top row is a Heart, your love affairs are favored; you will soon meet your mate. This situation is strengthened if the top row contains more Hearts than any other suit. If you are a woman, look out for the Queen of Hearts; if you are a man, take special notice of the King. These are important significators of meeting a mate.

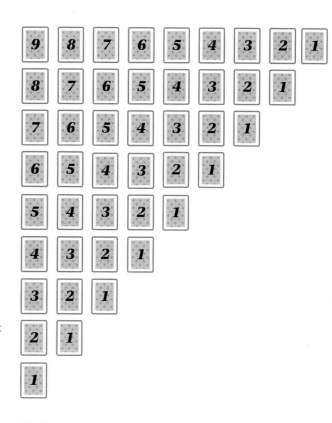

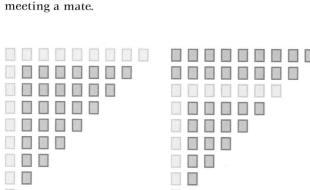 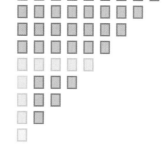 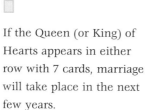

If you are single and the Queen (or King) of Hearts is placed in either row of 9 cards, you will meet your mate and marry very soon.

If the Queen (or King) of Hearts appears in either row with 7 cards, marriage will take place in the next few years.

If the Queen (or King) of Hearts appears in either row with 5 cards, marriage is not within the foreseeable future.

If the Queen (or King) of Hearts is one of the seven leftover cards, you may well meet your mate, but marriage is unlikely.

Dominoes

These not only can indicate if you are to meet someone special soon but also whether you will be lucky in love. Spread the dominoes face-side-down on a flat surface. Choose one. Check below to see the possible result if you've drawn one of the following:

 Six-Four Early marriage, children following quickly.

 Six-Three Marriage to a reliable person.

 Six-Two Excellent for love affairs; could indicate marriage.

 Five-Two Unrequited love.

 Five-One Short-lived affair.

 Double One or Two-Blank Needs work but partnership succeeds.

 Double Five Great success in love.

 Double Three A new lover is certain; an unexpected falling in love.

Runes

For thousands of years, runes have been used to foresee a lover. To find out whether you are going to meet one soon, simply put your hand into your rune pouch (see page 166) and pull one out. Look out for:

Teiwaz A new, high-octane love affair, not without danger, watch out!

Gebo Partnership.

Wunjo A fair haired man from overseas is breezing into your life.

If your rune isn't one of the favorable ones, don't despair; it just means someone isn't on the horizon just yet. You always can try again later. You can check any other rune for its meaning on pages 167–9.

Love Dots

The dots on a pair of dice can quickly tell you if you will soon find love. Concentrate on that question and roll the dice. See if your answer is one of the two below; if not, refer to the following pages to find more lucky dot combinations.

 Two Ones You'll be meeting your new lover tomorrow.

 One and Three You have to wait until your next social event.

Love Dots

Fortunes can be won or lost on a throw of the dice, but their dots also can be used to answer a variety of questions concerning love. A set formula of questions and answers quickly pinpoints the oracle's response. Anything with dots is suitable if you don't have dice handy. To use dominoes, set aside any with blanks, then select one at random. With playing cards, discard all those with a face value above 6, select two at random from the remainder and you have your answer.

Method

Select from the list of questions the one closest to your own. So, if you want to know if someone you met is going to ask you out, select question 2.

1 *Does the one I love think of me often?*
2 *Will I have a date soon?*
3 *How many lovers will I have?*
4 *How many times will I marry?*
5 *Does my lover love me?*
6 *Will I soon find love?*
7 *Will I marry soon?*
8 *Will I marry the person I am thinking of?*
9 *Which of my lovers is the right one?*

Concentrating on the question, shake and throw two dice (or pick a domino or two cards).
Read off the result from the table.

One and One

1 As often as you think of him/her.
2 At ll a.m. tomorrow.
3 More than twelve.
4 One.
5 S/he cannot avoid it.
6 Your heart is already engaged.
7 One week.
8 No.
9 The one with the longest nose.

One and Two

1 Never.
2 Yes, unfortunately for you.
3 As many lovers as husbands.
4 Twice.
5 Heart and soul.
6 Tomorrow.
7 Two years' time.
8 If you want to.
9 The darker one.

One and Three

1 Of course.
2 Yes, but with a rogue.
3 One, a great admirer.
4 Once.
5 Notice the blushes!
6 At your next social event.
7 Never.
8 Yes, and others.
9 The long-haired one.

One and Four

1 They do not dare.
2 If you don't worry.
3 Four or five.
4 Once, joyfully, to a "G."
5 Pass him/her a drink. Hand touches? Yes!
6 Your heart is not free.
7 Within a year.
8 Unlikely.
9 The one who touches you first.

One and Five

1 As often as possible.
2 When you have wrinkles.
3 Seven at least.
4 Once, to a good person.
5 As a brother or sister.
6 You love one now, but soon love another.
7 Within four years.
8 You know this is impossible.
9 The one who blushes.

Love Dots

(continued)

One and Six

1 Yes, but reluctantly.
2 You are better off if you don't.
3 Well over 20, five of whom love you already.
4 Three times.
5 His/her heart is faithful to another.
6 Your heart will not remain free much longer.
7 Only when you love more tenderly than now.
8 If s/he is not already engaged, yes.
9 The one with large ears.

Two and Two

1 All the time.
2 You are surrounded by admirers.
3 Five.
4 Once, to a jealous partner.
5 Look into his/her face.
6 5 p.m. tomorrow.
7 Six weeks' time.
8 Yes.
9 The shrewd one.

Two and Three

1 S/he is busy with other things.
2 Treat someone with more regard, then yes.
3 Many, but you will be bored.
4 Once, to a romantic, with the initial "B."
5 Absolutely.
6 You are already in love.
7 In five months.
8 Yes.
9 The one with large hands.

Two and Four

1 You know the answer is yes.
2 Yes, but s/he is not serious.
3 A fair and a dark one.
4 More than once but unhappily.
5 Yes but s/he loves several.
6 For a year but not longer.
7 In six years, be patient.
8 Yes, if you capture the heart within six weeks.
9 The more modest of the two.

Two and Five

1 All the time.
2 Yes but don't expect happiness.
3 Two, one an "L."
4 Once.
5 From the moment you met.
6 On the next journey you take.
7 Within two years.
8 A false friend interferes.
9 The one with the big mouth.

Two and Six

1 Often.
2 Yes, a humorous but unhandsome person.
3 Twelve or so.
4 Possibly once, maybe not at all.
5 With great longing.
6 In six weeks, in starlight.
7 In a year or two.
8 No.
9 The generous one.

Three and Three

1 Always and tenderly.
2 Quite a few.
3 An older man you don't care for.
4 Twice.
5 A true friend but that is all.
6 Very soon.
7 It will always be free.
8 If you truly love.
9 The least pretentious one.

Three and Four

1 Yes, but not as you would like.
2 Soon, more than you can accept.
3 Several, but mostly unattractive.
4 If you accept all proposals, more than you can count.
5 Yes, but believes you do not return the love.
6 You will be slow to give your heart.
7 Within one year.
8 To succeed, flirt less with others.
9 The one who agrees with you.

Three and Five

1 More often than you do.
2 With no one who is worth having.
3 Two, both good looking.
4 Once, and that is more than enough.
5 As often as possible.
6 Is your heart really free now?
7 Within three years.
8 This is not what you desire.
9 The well-mannered one.

Three and Six

1 Rarely and without love.
2 Yes, a sailor, heir to a fortune.
3 One rich, two poor.
4 Once to someone you dominate.
5 You are the first and only love.
6 For two more years.
7 Within five years.
8 Yes, happily ever after.
9 The first to profess love.

Four and Four

1 Lower your expectations.
2 Tomorrow, the first person you meet!
3 One. A fair-haired, slow person with a big mouth.
4 As many times as you have had lovers.
5 Yes.
6 You have been in love too often already.
7 In three to four years.
8 If not, it is not your fault.
9 The one with come-hither eyes.

Four and Five

1 Always.
2 Not for a long time.
3 A tall, slender, dark, and handsome person.
4 Once to a tyrant.
5 You cannot imagine how much.
6 Love will come soon, after unhappiness.
7 Within six years.
8 A bitter enemy prevents this.
9 The one who stumbles when next to you.

Four and Six

1 Yes, with affection.
2 Do you need to ask?
3 Three at least.
4 One tall, one medium, one short.
5 You are the light.
6 Soon you will fall for someone you could not stand.
7 Not for seven years.
8 Yes, but less happily than you hoped.
9 The fatter of the two.

Five and Five

1 Not as yet.
2 Someone is desperate to ask you out.
3 Three, one of whom's name begins with a "W."
4 Once, to a person whose name begins with "J" who you already know.
5 Secretly but it may never be said aloud.
6 A lover is not free at the moment, but will be soon.
7 This year.
8 S/he will never marry.
9 The one who laughs.

Five and Six

1 Yes, but there is bitterness.
2 Someone you meet within three days.
3 Two, one a distant relative.
4 Once, to the person you think most unlikely.
5 Faithfully and truly.
6 No, it will be stolen.
7 Before next winter.
8 Yes.
9 The snub-nosed one.

Six and Six

1 Yes, but is afraid of being carried away.
2 With an older person.
3 Quite a few, none seriously.
4 It would be better if none.
5 As much as you do.
6 Not for a year.
7 Never.
8 Persist, in the end success will come.
9 The one you met by chance.

Who will my lover be?

What will s/he look like?
How will I recognize him/her?

After asking: "Will I meet someone?," the next question is usually: "Who will it be?" Playing Cards can tell you. Traditionally, this form of divination was practiced by the female sex, but it is relevant to the male as well. Legend has it that playing cards arrived in Medieval Europe from the Middle East. At that time, a young girl called Odette loved King Charles VI of France, who suffered from periods of madness and deep depression. To distract him Odette sought out the colored cards that had recently arrived. With them came a Saracen woman who taught Odette to read the cards for divination. They soon became very popular but some courtiers were disconcerted to learn that they revealed their infidelities. Many people believe the cards to be much older, but one thing is certain, for at least eight centuries, cards have been used to symbolize lover and beloved.

Playing Cards

Certain cards represent a particular coloring. Hearts are the suit associated with love and the Knave (or Jack) of Hearts stole more than his fair share of hearts. He represents a young man (or woman) who is charming but not altogether to be trusted. The Jack of Spades, on the other hand, is the tall, dark, handsome stranger who sweeps a girl off her feet — not always with the best of intentions. If a picture card or an eight of hearts or clubs turns up in your reading, their human counterpart is sure to follow:

Method

You will need two full packs of playing cards.

- Shuffle each pack in turn.
- Cut the first pack and re-form.
- Cut the second pack and place the top card face up on the recombined pack.
- Taking the first pack, turn up until the card is reached that pairs with the card on top of the second pack.
- Turn five cards.

If one is a King, Queen, Jack, or the eight of hearts or clubs, read meaning as appropriate to your sex and sexual orientation. A Jack can mean a young woman and an eight can indicate a young man.

If no appropriate card is found, no one is waiting to meet you at present.

Hearts

King A sympathetic, professional middle-aged man whose hair is auburn or light brown. Pinkish tinge to complexion. Blue, gray, or hazel eyes.

Queen A pleasant, lively, good-looking woman often with fairish hair and pink complexion. Blue, gray, or hazel eyes.

Jack A pleasure-loving young man whose hair is fair or auburn. Blue, gray, or hazel eyes.

Eight An auburn haired young woman with blue, gray, or hazel eyes.

Clubs

King A practical, affectionate man of forty or over with brown or red hair. Florid or dark complexion, brown or hazel eyes.

Queen A dark, wealthy, amorous woman with a quick temper. High color or dark complexion with brown or hazel eyes.

Jack A clever, young, brown or red haired man, very much in love (reversed, a flirt). Eyes brown or hazel, complexion ruddy or dark skin.

Eight A dark haired young woman with hazel or brown eyes and high color or dark skin.

Diamonds

King A powerful, sophisticated, middle-aged man with light hair and fiery temper. Pale complexion, light blue or gray eyes.

Queen A spiteful, light haired, woman who is a stranger and a gossip. Light blue or gray eyes with pale complexion.

Jack A young man with light hair, blue or gray eyes and pale complexion. An unfaithful friend.

Spades

King A dark or gray haired man well past forty, possibly a widower. Sallow complexion with dark eyes.

Queen An affectionate dark haired widow or divorcee who wishes to remarry. Sallow complexion with dark eyes.

Jack A young dark haired man with sallow complexion. Eyes usually dark brown or dark blue. May be an insincere philanderer.

Are we compatible?

Will my romance last?
Can we work out our differences?

Compatibility is of great import. Just because you are attracted to someone, it does not mean you will get along with him or her. Relationships are often a compromise. You choose someone with whom you are basically compatible, but agree to differ at times. If you have insight into where you are different, then your prospects of maintaining a successful relationship increase. Problems arise when two fundamentally opposed approaches to life clash — and when one person expects the other to change or does not recognize a basic difference. With the blossoming of international travel, more and more people are wondering if summer romances will work out. There is a natural concern that someone from a different background may not be compatible. Over the years, different ways have been found to answer these questions. Palmistry can show if you will get along with a prospective partner as can Astrology — both Western and Eastern.

Palmistry

Your hand can reveal a surprising amount about your love life. It can tell how passionate you are and show whether you and someone else are compatible. If you are not familiar with all the major lines, see page 58.

Passionate Hands

If your hand has a strong Girdle of Venus you are passionate and intense about love — and could well be jealous. If the Mound of Venus is well developed, so are your libido and ability to express affection. If it is flat, you are cooler in love. With a healthy Heart Line, you enjoy a happy, long-term relationship. A very deep, red line indicates great passion — so much so that one partner is unlikely to be sufficient. Breaks or islands in your Heart Line can indicate affairs and separations.

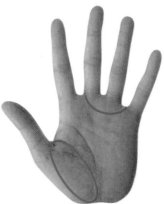

Passionate Hands have a strong Girdle of Venus and possibly a well-developed Mound of Venus.

Compatible Hands

As a general rule, the more alike hands are, the more a couple will get along. This particularly applies to patterns and lines on the hand. However, the shape of your hands says a great deal about you and the people with whom you are compatible (see opposite).

Psychic Hands denote great sensitivity. Incompatible with square or spatulate hands. With other psychic hands, find difficulty in handling everyday reality. Conic types best match.

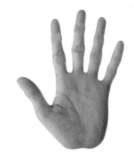

Philosophic Hands demonstrate intelligence. Benefit from practical partners. Impulsive conic hands confuse philosophic.

Conic Hands signify adaptability. Compatible with other conics and sensitive psychic hands.

Western Astrology

Traditionally, astrological signs which share the same element get on well together, while signs that are opposite attract — but all may not go smoothly!

♈ **Aries**
♉ **Taurus**
♊ **Gemini**
♋ **Cancer**
♌ **Leo**
♍ **Virgo**
♎ **Libra**
♏ **Scorpio**
♐ **Sagittarius**
♑ **Capricorn**
♒ **Aquarius**
♓ **Pisces**

● **Fire**
● **Earth**
● **Air**
● **Water**

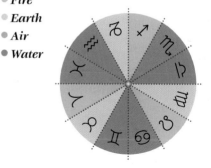

Square Hands indicate practicality. Compatible with other squares, creative spatulate hands and temperamental conic types.

Spatulate Hands point to a love of fresh air and exercise. This active hand is practical and is compatible with square hands but becomes impatient with dreamy psychic hands.

Chinese Astrology

Each year is assigned an animal. Some of the Chinese animals get along with almost everyone: enthusiastic, unpredictable Tigers, for instance, blend in with most other animals, although Tigers may quickly move on. Tiger energy, however, can be too inflammatory for another Tiger, or for timid Rabbit and Snake who like a quiet life. See overleaf for your compatible signs.

Chinese Astrology

The Chinese assign each year an animal. Each animal has specific characteristics, and everyone born in an animal year shares those characteristics. Animals are compatible with, or antithetical to, each other. People born under the same animal usually get along, and those who share similar approaches to life through sympathetic animal-alignments support each other. But there are combinations that just do not work well. A timid Rabbit, for instance, gets very nervous when faced with the drive and energy of a highly-charged Rat.

To find your animal, find your year of birth below. If you were born in late January or early February, you could well belong to the animal of the preceding year (see page 182 for a complete listing).

The main characteristics of the animals in love are set out opposite. To find out how you get along with other animals, see far right and overleaf.

Rat	1912	1924	1936	1948	1960	1972	1984	1996
Ox	1913	1925	1937	1949	1961	1973	1985	1997
Tiger	1914	1926	1938	1950	1962	1974	1986	1998
Rabbit	1915	1927	1939	1951	1963	1975	1987	1999
Dragon	1916	1928	1940	1952	1964	1976	1988	2000
Snake	1917	1929	1941	1953	1965	1977	1989	2001
Horse	1918	1930	1942	1954	1966	1978	1990	2002
Ram	1919	1931	1943	1955	1967	1979	1991	2003
Monkey	1920	1932	1944	1956	1968	1980	1992	2004
Rooster	1921	1933	1945	1957	1969	1981	1993	2005
Dog	1922	1934	1946	1958	1970	1982	1994	2006
Pig	1923	1935	1947	1959	1971	1983	1995	2007

Rat Highly charged. Emotionally labile. Faithful. Passionate, attentive. Strong desire for security. Needs complete involvement, commitment. Must be part of partner's plans. Easily hurt if ignored.

Rabbit Searching for soulmate. Values security, trust, affection. Needs intimacy and stability. Withdraws if partner erratic or over-demanding. Nervous, insecure. Listens but does not reveal.

Ox Cautious approach to love. Needs strong love, support and commitment. Emotionally dependable. Reluctant to experiment, can be persuaded to have fun. Tolerant partner, does not blame other.

Dragon Charismatic, flirtatious, exuberant. Emotional game-player. Difficulty settling down, has affairs. Dislikes emotional dependency or indecision. Needs space and understanding partner.

Tiger Enthusiastic, active. Changeable. Emotionally honest. Enjoys variety — hates predictability or boredom. Moves on fast. Appreciates independent, adventurous partner.

Snake Seductive, beguiling, secretive. Does not let go. Romantic, loving, humorous partner but jealous, possessive. Needs space. Flirts, but guards partner. Cherishes intimate moments.

Horse Tempestuous, impetuous. Easily carried away. Loves thrill of new romance. Difficulty settling down but serious about commitment. Needs freedom, nurturing, and reassurance. Loving partner.

Rooster Independent, restless, charming. Enjoys romance. Easily bored, moves on quickly. When finally settled, deeply committed and attentive. Hidden jealous streak. Reliable partner.

Ram Security orientated. Unconventional, creative. Highly emotional, difficulty expressing feelings. Initially shy. Dislikes being dominated. Romantic, seeks protection. May hurt others.

Dog Strong desire for security. Encourages partner to share difficulties, but avoids sharing own. Faithful, loyal, affectionate. If hurt, needs time to rebuild trust. Sees criticism where none intended.

Monkey Romantic, lively, excitable. Difficulty in commiting. Initially nervous and insecure, but faithful, supportive, and dependable when established. Remains an excellent friend.

Pig Sensitive, fun loving. Tolerant, resilient. Naive emotionally; may be taken advantage of. Trusting partner, but needs romance before settling down to love. Too many demands: feels trapped.

The Love Combinations

Rat and Rat Inflammatory. Initially consumed by each other. Passionate and intense, sharing fun. Understand other's need to keep secrets, but suspicious. Too similar to last?

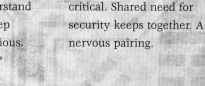

Rat and Rabbit Tenuous. Rat's unpredictability challenges timid Rabbit. Danger of Rat being over-critical. Shared need for security keeps together. A nervous pairing.

Rat and Ox Complementary, mutual respect. Ox deals with daily affairs, Rat initiates ideas. Ox's common sense backs Rat's astuteness. Rat's passion enlivens Ox. Ox anchor for Rat. Enduring.

Rat and Dragon Lively and adventurous. Dragon charms rat while holding center stage. Rat massages Dragon's ego. Gregarious and open, allow each other space. Enduring.

Rat and Tiger Shared need for change, constant stimulation. Tiger more adventurous and Tiger's flirtations threaten Rat. Tiger needs to understand Rat's security needs. Endures if handled well.

Rat and Snake Stimulating. Mutual telepathy. Acute observers, grab opportunities. Shared sense of humor — and passion. Snake takes longer to commit, Rat must wait. Enduring.

Love Combinations (continued)

Rat and Horse
Emotionally absorbed. Intense and passionate — until Rat pulls back. Conflicts develop: Horse absorbed in relationship, Rat outside interests. To endure, Rat curbs criticism.

Rat and Rooster
Initially superficial, deepens if first impressions overcome. Rat first observes Rooster as flamboyant and shallow, but comes to appreciate honest Rooster. Enduring.

Ox and Ox
Stable partnership. Excellent organizers, choosing security over risk. Mutual aims. Prefer cool emotions, avoid turbulence. If too predictable, one throws caution to winds.

Ox and Dragon
Challenging. Ox patient, predictable, cautious; Dragon fiery and spontaneous. Dragon likes Ox's dependability, Ox enthused by Dragon's energy. Mutual understanding needed.

Rat and Ram
Challenging. Rat more energetic than Ram, who cannot be pushed. Share determined streak. Rat seeks recognition, Ram introspection. To thrive, Rat needs tolerance, Ram focus.

Rat and Dog
Trusting bond. Watch each other's back. Shared need for privacy. Rat's social confidence allays Dog's anxieties. Dog fearlessly supports Rat. Relationship thrives.

Ox and Tiger
Somewhat tricky. Balance between Tiger's itchy feet and Ox's desire for stability. Tiger provides security if Ox avoids dependence. Needs mutual trust.

Ox and Snake
Balanced combination. Dependable Ox takes care of domestic details, charming Snake goes into world and returns to be nurtured. If trust issue resolved, lasting, stable partnership.

Rat and Monkey
Competitive. Both strong and energetic, Monkey gains upper hand. Rat's passion too intense for controlled and emotionally manipulative Monkey. To endure, space needed.

Rat and Pig
Deep, loving relationship. Pig copes with Rat's passion and moods, but aggression disturbs equilibrium. Shared fun and mutual indulgence. Pig's naivety frustrating.

Ox and Rabbit
Home-loving combination. Do not want risks or emotional turbulence. Stable Ox gives Rabbit security. If Ox too fixed, Rabbit brings about compromise. Lasting.

Ox and Horse
Opposites attract. Ox plods, restless Horse gallops ahead. Ox compromises and offers patient support. If Ox expects Horse to behave sensibly, disappointment follows.

Ox and Ram Mutually supportive. Ox provides stability, Ram provides ideas. Ox taking over organization and decision making relieves Ram. Ox may be too predictable. Lasting.

Ox and Dog Loyal and faithful. Shared bond. Dog becomes anxious about future, Ox deals with immediate problems while planning ahead. Ox calms Dog, appreciates faithfulness. Lasting.

Tiger and Rabbit Both need secure home base but Tiger more adventurous and most likely to leave. Rabbit needs time alone. Can work well if intimate moments are shared.

Tiger and Horse Lively. Shared passion for life. Seek new avenues together. Tiger does not notice Horse's egoism and unconscious self-centeredness so relationship flourishes.

Ox and Monkey Trusting and balanced. Lively monkey involved with projects, Ox stays out of Monkey's games, cares for home. Ox's thoroughness appeals to Monkey. If no deception, lasting.

Ox and Pig Mutually supportive. Ox enjoys Pig's playfulness, acquiesces to demands. Clash between social life (Pig) and home life (Ox) — and when Pig overspends. Stable, enduring.

Tiger and Dragon High-spirited and passionate. Far from dull, arguments are relished. Sociable — always ready to explore new possibilities. Lasting duo.

Tiger and Ram Independence, interdependence. Both need space: Tiger for new interests, Ram for contemplation. Tiger provides Ram with security. Lasting when neither feels trapped.

Ox and Rooster Happy balance. Share privacy and freedom. Respect other's talents. Rooster livens up Ox. Ox provides emotional security and support for Rooster's less way-out ideas, diverts unrealistic.

Tiger and Tiger Inflammatory. Independent and determined, neither gives way. Both need freedom to pursue other interests. Will work with sufficient space.

Tiger and Snake Tricky. Come from different places. Tiger too adventurous for routine-loving Snake. Share ideas and socializing. Compromise needed.

Tiger and Monkey Happy combination. Astute and adventurous, enjoy new possibilities. Monkey controls relationship. Work well together. Tiger has to cultivate patience, Monkey openness and honesty.

Tiger and Rooster
Initially exciting. Tiger's attention caught by Rooster's outgoing nature, but becomes critical. Misunderstandings arise. Patience and openness about needs and feelings required.

Rabbit and Rabbit
Harmonious. Share need for calmness and peace. Content with each other. Enjoy beautiful surroundings, familiar environment. Keep an eye to future to avoid unpleasant surprises.

Rabbit and Horse Very loving. Mutually supportive. Horse supplies passion and affection Rabbit desires, and reassures about love. Rabbit supports Horse on "down days." Lasting partnership.

Rabbit and Rooster
Opposite extremes. Rabbit too placid for Rooster. Rooster too boisterous for Rabbit. Rabbit needs to appreciate hidden, sensitive side of Rooster, Rooster to trust Rabbit.

Tiger and Dog Mutually formidable. Good team. Tiger is impetuous, Dog more cautious. Tiger appreciates Dog's watchfulness, Dog prevents Tiger going too far. To last, Dog needs displays of affection.

Rabbit and Dragon
Opposing needs. Dragon looks for challenge and adventure, cautious Rabbit security and reassurance. Rabbit admires Dragon's confidence and lets Dragon take center stage.

Rabbit and Ram
Soulmates. Happily share experiences. Ram calms Rabbit's nervousness. Rabbit offers security when Ram nervous. When both face problems, work on them together.

Rabbit and Dog Reliable partnership. Both honorable and honest. Never compromise security. Defend and comfort each other. Rabbit keeps peace in lasting relationship.

Tiger and Pig Mutually supportive. Shared interests. Great friendship. Balances need for companionship with independence, allow each other space. Lasting.

Rabbit and Snake Two home lovers escape into paradise. Enjoy each other's company. Rabbit needs more privacy than Snake but Snake opens Rabbit up to the world outside. Snake needs to practice tolerance.

Rabbit and Monkey
Caring partnership. Rabbit aware of Monkey's games, keeps them in check. Monkey appreciates Rabbit's astuteness. Compromise possible. Two grow together.

Rabbit and Pig Peaceful combination. Mutual hopes and aims. Spend time in conversation. Rabbit controls Pig's occasional rashness, keeps relationship on track. Enduring.

Dragon and Dragon
Powerful combination. Great attraction. Secure within relationship. Both active and vital, need attention from others. Share many possibilities but pursue them independently too.

Dragon and Ram
Exciting, but can be too fast for Ram. Dragon has many skills but Ram forgets the compliments Dragon requires. Dragon needs a listener, is Ram paying attention?

Dragon and Dog
Not a happy combination. Dog finds Dragon overwhelming and annoying. Faithful Dog needs to know where s/he stands, inconsistent Dragon overlooks inconvenient detail.

Snake and Horse
Devious. Snake subtly controls Horse who mistakenly feels in charge. Horse over-enthusiastic but Snake allows freedom while admiring from afar.

Dragon and Snake
Partnership of equals. Neither is intimidated by other. Snake allows Dragon a moment of glory, and congratulates or consoles, but can be possessive.

Dragon and Monkey
Ideal partnership. Two astute signs spark each other off. Dragon's bright attractiveness is no threat to Monkey — who can flatter Dragon's need for admiration.

Dragon and Pig
Supportive combination. Pig is happy to be swept along in Dragon's wake — and to provide the reassurance this insecure animal needs. Dragon allows Pig freedom.

Snake and Ram
Interesting combination. Shared dislike of routine and pressure. Snake disappears if circumstances do not suit — Ram does not notice. Avoid outside interests that are over-demanding.

Dragon and Horse
Shared enthusiasms. Both enjoy exploring, dislike practicalities or emotional demands. Dragon's desire for attention can make Horse feel trapped. Horse must be truthful.

Dragon and Rooster
Fun-loving partnership with a more serious side. Dragon's confidence boosts Rooster, who needs to share insecurities with close partner. Honesty pays off.

Snake and Snake
Mutual admiration society. Two wily, beguiling beings debating, sharing and planning together. Two determined minds, one could be oppressed. Do you know each other too well?

Snake and Monkey
Energetic combination. Monkey spots opportunities, Snake examines implications. Monkey impatient with Snake's seriousness. Monkey hard to pin down, be straightforward.

Love Combinations *(continued)*

Snake and Rooster
Stylish combination, natural empathy. Open and trusting. Elegant and interesting couple, shop together. Attraction runs deep, Snake recognizes Rooster's hidden attributes.

Horse and Horse Fast-paced. Passionate and romantic. If interest wanes, heads off to new pastures. Reassurance needed for inner doubts; should try to restore confidence rather than running away.

Horse and Rooster
Superficial similarities. Competitive, need to make an impression. Rooster critical, Horse impetuous. Mutual understanding and patience needed, with intimate moments.

Ram and Ram Natural empathy. Pair of dreamers, lack practicality. Can tolerate space and being close. Understand mutual need for spiritual dimension. Need practical working arrangement.

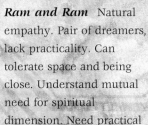

Snake and Dog Loyal combination. Dog admires Snake's intelligence and judgment, accepts advice. Snake soothes Dog's fears. Dog gives loyal background support to Snake.

Horse and Ram Happy adventurers. Unpredictable and lively. Horse may be too wrapped up in self to notice Ram needs encouragement from time to time. Can work well.

Horse and Dog Trusted partners. Faithful Dog gives Horse freedom to adventure, and patiently provides support at home. Dog is practical but pessimistic. Works if trust not abused.

Ram and Monkey
Indulgent companions. Enjoy travel and luxury. Monkey is supportive and constructive partner for insecure Ram. Monkey takes care of organizational detail.

Snake and Pig Happy combination. Pig enjoys Snake's tales, but if Snake wanders too often, Pig rebels. Snake jealous if Pig pursues much needed freedom. Trust required.

Horse and Monkey
Settles into surprisingly steady relationship. Initially, Horse's emotional intensity and commitment too much for Monkey. When understanding develops, happiness grows.

Horse and Pig Great playmates. Both show feelings honestly. Pig does not mind horse being selfish. Independent Pig needs breathing space, Horse must not be too demanding of attention.

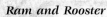

Ram and Rooster
Interesting, for a while. Rooster more forceful than Ram, who needs space. Ram needs to focus sympathy on Rooster, Rooster makes allowances for Ram's dreams.

Ram and Dog Mutually supportive with interest in the weird. Ram takes this further. Dog likes to remain in control, Ram gets carried away by dreams. If mutually depressed, need to inject optimism.

Monkey and Rooster Entertaining couple, share love of good life. Monkey more wily than Rooster, who needs to be center of attention. Monkey's games confuse Rooster. Tolerance needed.

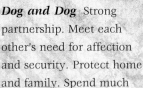 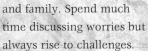

Rooster and Rooster Admire and annoy each other in equal measure. Criticism can be unintentionally hurtful. Recognize each other's vulnerability and need for support.

Dog and Dog Strong partnership. Meet each other's need for affection and security. Protect home and family. Spend much time discussing worries but always rise to challenges.

Ram and Pig Sensitive combination. Relate to each other well. Enjoy the arts together. Pig's practicality backs up Ram's creativity and calms tensions. Long-lasting support.

Monkey and Dog Uneasy combination. Tricky Monkey ducks and dives, Dog feels left out and unsure. Both critical and unlikely to be carried away by passion. Relationship needs openness.

Rooster and Dog Protective partners when relationship matures. Dog can be irritated by Rooster's need to perform but recognizes underlying sensitivity and provides support.

Dog and Pig Excellent understanding. When Dog is suspicious, Pig reassures. When Pig is in trouble, Dog protects. Dog can become morose and needlessly anxious but Pig sorts it out.

Monkey and Monkey Clever combination. Charm and captivate each other. Game-players, cannot fool each other. May become bored. Strong partnership that works well on shared projects.

Monkey and Pig Loyal partnership. Pig amused by Monkey's games, tolerantly observing from side. Pig provides good company and support for Monkey but can be manipulative.

Rooster and Pig Mutual support and friendship. Independence and companionship. Pig listens to Rooster's concerns and enjoys the entertainment Rooster provides.

Pig and Pig Tempestuous but enduring. Can gauge each other's moods and understand reasons. Share freedom and joint activities. May become dull, spice it up to last.

Is s/he really the one for me?

Do I fancy him/her?
Is s/he really interested?
Am I wasting my time?
Will this love be successful?

Having found a partner, there are many insecurities that can arise before a relationship comes to fruition. Doubts can set in. The secret is to disentangle what actually is from what you fear might be. Simple body language often gives you a clue to where a relationship will go. Is there hidden ambivalence? Your body will soon tell you! The modern world has forgotten its omens but the ancients saw meaning in the smallest thing. Keep your eyes open and you will become aware of how inanimate objects can speak. Check the opposite page to see whether some unexpected omen may indicate if this is the man or woman for you.

Body Language

You may not have noticed, but your body speaks your mind. Every gesture you make, every stance you take, indicates how you really feel about something. To know where a relationship is going, check out the body language.

This is the one for me!

The more you mirror each other, the more in accord you are. The more often you glance into each other's eyes, the more emotional contact you make. Legs crossed toward each other? Bodies held the same way? Heads tilted so as not to miss a word? Hands touching affectionately? Eyes only for each other? Looks like love!

I don't know...

Ambivalence makes itself known in little things. Arm around shoulder but head turned away. One leg pointing toward her, the other sliding off. He's attracted but he's terrified of being tied down. Is she really the one for him? She is leaning toward him at the top, but her legs are ready to walk away. Dependence and independence are battling it out. Can she trust him?

No way!

Do exactly the opposite of your partner and hidden tensions in your relationship are revealed. Legs crossed away from each other, eyes anywhere but on the beloved, hand over mouth or ear? These are clear signals that you do not care for what is being said, and want to be somewhere else — or your partner does.

Omens of Love

If a **needle breaks** when you are sewing, a young man is thinking of you.

If a **whole box of matches is spilt,** you can expect an early marriage. Any matches that remain in the box indicate the number of days, weeks, months, or years you will have to wait for marriage.

If you are **given a ring,** it is a token of love.

If the **ring breaks** you will separate. If the **ring is misshapen,** there is danger of betrayal.

If you **break a pair of scissors,** an argument or separation lies ahead.

If you **find a horseshoe** with your lover, you will find complete happiness.

If you **slip on a fruit skin,** you can expect a flirtation.

If you **slip in water,** look forward to love and tears.

If you accidentally **knock your hand against wood,** you will be loved. If you do the same **against iron,** do not trust your lover.

Stung by a bee and passion will soon be yours; by a **wasp** and you are in danger; by an **ant** and you will quarrel.

If you break glass, white glass is a good omen, red glass indicates worries to come, green glass means hope disappointed, and if you **break a glass full of wine,** you will find lasting love.

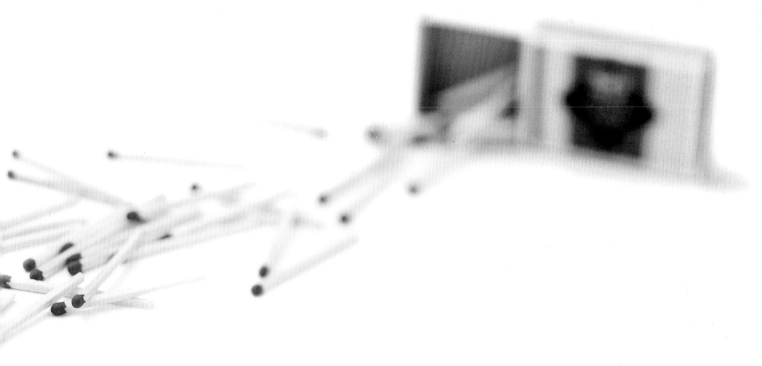

Can I trust my partner?

Do I have a rival?
Is my partner faithful?
Is s/he married?

Doubts arising in relationships may have more to do with yourself than your partner. The important thing is to determine if there really is something to worry about. Palmistry can help here. Your hand and that of your partner, can help to reassure you that your fears about relationship problems are groundless, or can confirm that you are right to be concerned. If you suspect you have a rival, check your hand first to ensure that you do not have a jealous streak causing you to see problems where none exist. Possessiveness will drive a loving partner away. If you are aware of this, you may be able to control your tendency to jealousy.

But there may be real problems that prevent the relationship from going further — your intended may be married or committed to another. Palmistry can help you find out the truth. The Hand of Fatima can tell you whether you will prevail over a known rival, while Dowsing can help to pinpoint an unknown one.

Palmistry

Your heart line will give you lots of information about how you view and react to love. Check to see whether you have a jealous hand. If insecurity centers around whether your lover is free to marry, your own hand will tell you if you are being deceived. A quick glance at your lover's hand may reveal the flirt and philanderer, or an unfaithful lover.

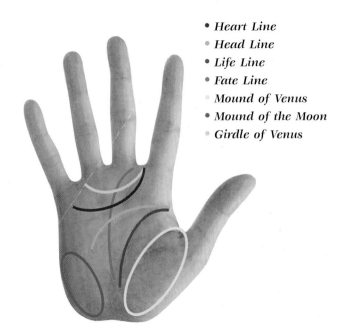

- **Heart Line**
- **Head Line**
- **Life Line**
- **Fate Line**
- **Mound of Venus**
- **Mound of the Moon**
- **Girdle of Venus**

The Heart Line

A clear line points to expectations of a faithful relationship. If the line is broken, chained or fragmented, then your expectation is of difficulty and emotional trauma. Thin and weak, you have little true desire for love. Line tilts up toward your middle finger, you create problems by placing your partner on a pedestal.

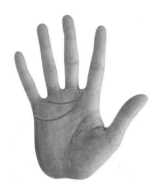

The Jealous Hand
Look at your palm to see if your Heart Line ends between your first and second fingers and also if your Girdle of Venus is solid. These are signs of jealousy — the fear is unnecessary and can push a faithful lover away.

A Married Lover?
An Influence Line heads toward your Fate Line, but a trellis gets in the way. There is an impediment to commitment.

The Hand of Fatima
If you know you have a rival, you can consult the Table of Numerical Victories below. The Hand of Fatima quickly pinpoints the victor in love as in any rivalry. Compute the value of both your name and that of your rival from the Wheel below the Hand (see page 30), and divide each by 9. The remainder is the number to use. For example, Judy equates to 7 and a suspected rival, Denise, would be 2. When 7 is asking the question, it prevails over 2, so I would be reassured.

Table of Numerical Victories

1	overcomes	2	3	7	9
2	overcomes	1	4	6	8
3	overcomes	2	5	7	9
4	overcomes	1	3	6	8
5	overcomes	2	4	7	9
6	overcomes	1	3	5	7
7	overcomes	2	4	6	8
8	overcomes	1	3	5	7
9	overcomes	2	4	6	8

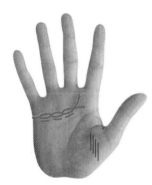

The Unfaithful Hand
Look at your lover's hand. An island in the middle of the Heart Line with chains and small lines? Vertical lines on the Mound of Venus? Infidelity is on the cards.

The Flirt & Philanderer
If your lover's hand displays many small lines feathering from the Heart Line, and cross-hatching on the Mound of Venus, s/he is revealed to be untrustworthy in love.

Pendulum Dowsing
Once you've programmed your pendulum (see page 137), you can use it to identify your rival. Write down a list of suspects. The pendulum will soon indicate who the culprit is.

Palmistry

Palmistry is divided into two areas: chirognomy (character analysis) and chiromancy (divination by the hand). Most people use a mixture of the two. Palmistry can tell you many things about your future: prospective partners, whether you will have a happy marriage or divorce, how many children you will have, whether your work is compatible, where health problems may lie — and a whole host of other information.

 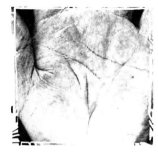

Right Hand

This is a palm print of a left handed person, so this hand shows "the fate" at birth.

Left Hand

This print shows the changes that have occurred as life has progressed, note the longer Life Line.

To read your own palm, make a hand print. The easiest way is to take a photocopy. Both hands are significant. If you are right-handed, your left hand usually shows the characteristics you were born with, and the right hand what you have made of them.

The major lines are the Heart, Head, Life, and Fate but all lines have significance.

One hand will often differ totally from the other, and the lines themselves can change over quite a short span of time. Future possibilities show up.

Timing

The Fate Line provides a rough guide when events happen. Working up from the base of Fate Line, the point level with base of thumb corresponds to age 23. The Fate Line crosses Head Line at around age 30, and Heart Line at about age 42. If Fate Line is strongest in early years, then the inquirer is ruled by fate in the first part of life, but free will takes over as s/he matures. If the fate line is strong at the top of palm, the inquirer will increasingly feel that fate has taken over.

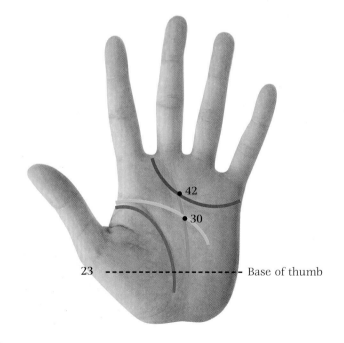

42

30

23 - Base of thumb

Should I make a commitment?

Should we get married?
Should we live together?

Now comes the great decision. Is this really Mr. or Ms. Right? Is it time for commitment? In years gone by, that almost inevitably meant marriage. Today it may mean living together, either because the parties prefer it that way, or because the nature of the relationship means that a legal ceremony is not possible. If you consult the oracle, make sure you do so in accord with your beliefs on this matter. It is no good asking the oracle if you should live together to please your partner, when you yearn for marriage. Differing attitudes, and different expectations, often underlie divorce, as does a too hasty jump into marriage. The oracle may well suggest a trial period of living together to see if you are really suited before you tie the knot.

Sun Signs
Different astrological signs have differing needs for commitment — or freedom. Some need marriage, others are happier living together. One sign will want to be very sure, another will rush in without thinking. Some are naturally faithful, others are not. Some have more staying power than others. Certain signs take divorce lightly, others resist parting under any circumstances.

 < None > Aries Passionate and spontaneous. Falls in love easily — always knows best. Moves in together quickly; out rapidly when things go wrong — usually in a temper. Happily marries. Usually faithful, not always.

 Taurus Sensual and stubborn. Takes time to consider. Marriage practical rather than romantic. Needs commitment, status, and security. Faithful. Jealous. Reluctant to divorce — stays unless extreme provocation.

 Gemini Charming and flirtatious. Hard to pin down. Commitment phobic. Prefers to live together but may talk him or herself into marriage. Several affairs. Talks things over but divorces quickly and moves on.

 Cancer Home loving and sensitive. Slow to commit. Many romances. Seeks security, prefers marriage. Keeps feelings hidden. Usually faithful. Divorce: holds on to bitter end.

 Leo Passionate and flamboyant. Likes to be courted into saying "yes." Enjoys big wedding but may live with partner first. Reasonably faithful when the center of attention. Divorces only after extreme provocation.

 Virgo Discriminating and fastidious. Takes things slowly. Perfectionist. Analyzes feelings. Strong romantic ideals. May live together until absolutely sure but once committed, that's it. Faithful. Divorces reluctantly.

Libra Charming and compliant. Needs relationship. Prefers marriage but lives together if only way to get relationship. Partner pleaser. Flirtations, affairs possible. Divorce unlikely.

Scorpio Sexy and intense. Moves in slowly. Fixed; values commitment and faithfulness, not necessarily marriage. Mates for life. Secretive. Extreme jealousy may provoke partner to divorce.

Sagittarius Spontaneous and freedom-loving. Falls happily in — and out — of love. Prefers live-in relationships with space. Dislikes commitment, may have affairs. Believes grass is greener elsewhere. Discusses feelings. Divorces speedily.

Capricorn Conventional and cautious. Falls in love slowly. Can be control-freak. Needs stability, commitment, marriage. Strong sex-drive; affairs but marriage goes on. Divorces reluctantly.

Aquarius Unconventional and zany. Difficult to predict. Paradox: needs commitment and freedom. Chooses unconventional lifestyle. Sexually inventive. Settles late, lives together first. Faithful. Divorces when bored.

Pisces Dreamy and romantic. In love with love. Drifts in and out of affairs. Rarely ends one before beginning another. Unfaithful. Leaves and returns. Divorces reluctantly, may marry several times.

What Gets in the Way of Love?

Romantic notions of love often get in the way of real love. Romantic love may be great for an affair, but it is not a good base for a permanent relationship. Too much idealism, too high an expectation of what love is, seeking "the one," looking to a partner to make you feel complete — these are all attitudes that can defeat love.

Expectations and fears, too, can get in the way of even the most blissful attraction. If relationships have gone badly in the past, the baggage will be carried forward as expectations. As we create what we most fear, if you believe things will go wrong, they will do so. If you feel insecure inside, you may wonder how anyone could possibly love you. A "fault" may be a good get-out for you. Just because you are looking for love, it does not mean that you are not afraid of commitment!

Knowing yourself well helps you find out what is getting in the way — and the more profound oracles soon tell you, if you are willing to hear. As many of the barriers to love are located out of sight in your subconscious mind, you may be quite shocked as to what the oracle comes up with. Do not dismiss it out of hand. Test it out and phrase your questions carefully for maximum insight.

Daisies

Plucking petals is a time-honored way to find out the answer to: "S/he loves me, s/he loves me not" and similar questions. Use this "field" of odd and even-petaled daisies to find your answer.

Closing your eyes, touch one of the flowers. Then open your eyes and count the petals. A flower with an even number of petals equals "No;" one with odd-numbered petals means "Yes."

Palmistry

Marriage Lines are found on the outside edge of your palm beneath the little finger. You may need to move your finger forward to see them clearly. They do not necessarily indicate marriage; a stable, committed relationship shows as a Marriage Line. The deeper the line, the happier the relationship. A Marriage Line low on the hand indicates an early wedding; high, a commitment later in life. If a Marriage Line suddenly turns upward toward your little finger, there is a bar to legal marriage. In some hands, lines on the palm form an "M," a particularly significant indicator of happy marriage. The "M" is formed from the Head, Heart, Life, and Success Lines uniting to form a clear letter as illustrated.

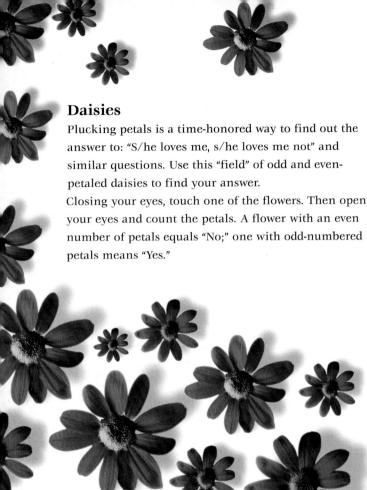

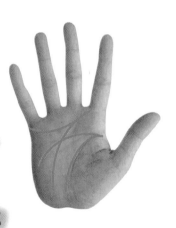
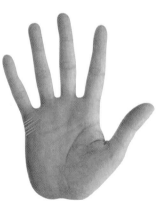

The **"M"** shows clearly and is formed from the head, heart, life, and success lines uniting.

Marriage Lines are found on the outside edge of your palm beneath the little finger.

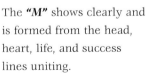

Dominoes

For a fast answer as to whether to commit yourself or not, spread a box of dominoes face down on a table. Concentrate on your question and turn one domino face up.

 Double Six A definite Yes!

Other answers may be negative or more equivocal, see full meanings on pages 114–15.

I Ching

This Chinese oracle has been consulted for thousands of years to find answers to life's important questions. Its answers are coded under hexagrams — six-lined figures, each of which has a particular meaning. To create a hexagram, you will need a pencil and paper and three coins. Take the coins and throw them on a table in front of you. Starting at the bottom of the hexagram and building up, draw an unbroken (yang) line every time you see a majority of heads. Draw a broken (yin) line every time you see a majority of tails. Throw the coins six times in all; you will have created a hexagram. If your hexagram is one of the following, these are definite indications of unity and partnership. If you've drawn either of these, commitment will soon follow.

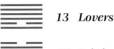 *13 Lovers*

45 Joining Together

For other hexagrams, see pages 66–69.

When Is a Good Day to Get Married?

Playing Cards

A pack of cards can help you pick your day but you also need an almanac showing new moon dates. Most diaries and calendars carry this information.

Method
- Shuffle, cut and re-form the pack.
- Deal the pack, picking out the seventh, ninth and twelfth cards. Put the others aside.

Consult an almanac to ascertain the dates of the new moon in each month. The seventh, ninth and twelfth days after the new moon are auspicious days. Therefore, if you are thinking of a day in June and the new moon falls on the 3rd of June, for example, the 10th, 12th and 15th of June will be auspicious days.

To find the most propitious day for your wedding, look at the three cards you removed from the deck. Hearts are most desirable, followed by clubs, diamonds, and spades. In order of preference, therefore, if one of your cards is a heart, choose the day it represents. If hearts is the seventh card, then you would choose the seventh day after the new moon or June 10th, similarly if it is the ninth card, you would choose June 12th and if it is the twelfth card, you should pick June 15. If you don't have a heart, look next for clubs followed by diamonds and finally spades, and work out the dates of the cards. If you have two or more cards of the same suit, the days they represent will be equally fortunate.

Is it over?

Will s/he come back?

Should I break off the affair?

Is there a chance of reconciliation?

The sad day may arrive when the romance, or the marriage appears to be over. Most people take being deserted badly. Self image is knocked off balance, inner security threatened. Questions arise. "Is this really the end?" A quick answer can be obtained with dominoes, dice, runes and playing cards — if your pick isn't indicated, the answer is not straightforward! Your palm also can reveal the answer.

And what if you're unsure why the affair is over? The I Ching is an ancient, if enigmatic, aid to understanding not only what will happen but why something has occurred.

Dominoes

If you are wondering if your romance is over and any of the following appear when you select a domino from the face down set spread out on the table, you will have your answer.

 Double Blank Misfortune ahead. Be warned!

 Six-One The end of all your dreams.

 Four-Blank Temporary reconciliation.

 Four-Two Domestic upheavals. Beware of a flirt or philanderer.

Playing Cards

Certain cards have always been considered unlucky; Spades do not auger well for the future and one in particular can spell the end when upside down in a spread (if your pack has no clear "up," mark one corner as the top). If a card appears the other way up, it is reversed.

Eight of Spades (Reversed) A broken engagement or marriage.

Dice

The roll of the dice can bring good or bad fortune. For a quick answer as to whether it's over or not, roll a single die:

 Five Trouble and strife.

Runes

Sometimes your subconscious mind knows more than you do. Runes are one way of tuning into its knowledge and drawing one from your rune pack (see pages 166–9) will quickly pinpoint what is in store for you. Check whether your rune is the right way up (upright) or reversed (upside down) as the meaning may change:

Hagalaz A bolt from the blue.

Eihwaz Upright: Remain flexible. Reversed: Vacillation.

Teiwaz Reversed: For a man, broken love affair. For a woman, obsessive relationship.

Berkhana Reversed: plans not reaching fruition.

Kano Divorce.

Othila Separation.

I Ching

Throwing coins enables you to access the wisdom of this ancient Chinese oracle. Follow the instructions overleaf and you will be warned of impending separation or to expect reconciliation. Look out for

  2 Passive Acceptance.

  8 Unity.

  40 Disentangling.

  21 Biting Through.

  24 Turning Point.

  18 Work on What Is Spoiled.

Turn the page to learn more.

I Ching

*According to one legend, over five thousand years ago,
the Emperor Fu Hsi was meditating by a river bank
when a dragon-horse rose out of the water. Entranced by
the beautiful patterns its scales formed, Fu Hsi conceived
the oracular system known as the I Ching, or Book of
Changes. Over the centuries it developed from a handful
of basic hexagrams (six-lined figures) into a complex and
accurate system of divination. Today the I Ching forms
one of the five classics of Chinese philosophy, as highly
regarded in the East as the Bible is in the West. It is
probably the oldest continually used oracle in existence.*

Method

In China, yarrow stalks were used to create the
hexagrams. This was a long and laborious
process as it was thought to concentrate the mind
and make it receptive to the answer. Nowadays it is
more usual to employ three coins to cast the
hexagrams, and it is possible to use ordinary coins
as long as they have clear "heads" and "tails."

- Throw three coins onto the table in front of you.

- Heads represents a yang or unbroken line ———.
  Tails represents a yin or broken line — —. Mostly
  heads forms a yang line; tails a yin line.

- Write the line down, leaving space above for five
  more lines.

- Throw the coins five times more until you have
  created your hexagram, writing bottom to top.

- Identify your hexagram on the following pages; its
  meaning will be your answer.

1 Creative Action Take action, result favorable. Persist, do not push too hard. Potential lover needs time.

2 Passive Acceptance Do not force, allow flow to bring desired outcome. Future in hands of others. Let go old love, new one emerges.

3 Gestation Take action slowly, things evolving. Handle with care. Look to others for guidance. Find yourself before loving.

4 Growth Matters at immature stage. If no success, try again. Try change of direction. Help from wisdom of others.

5 Calculated Inaction Danger ahead, pause. Go slowly, especially in love. Savor moment. Promise of future success. Friends aid you.

6 Conflict Matters do not go well. Unfair blame. Allies turn into enemies. Do not argue. Take time to talk. Wait until things improve.

7 Battle Fight or opposition to face. Be determined. Take control. Fight or retreat, you choose. Guidance near at hand. Military involvement possible.

8 Unity Successful partnership. Peace and harmony. Fragmented relationship reunites. Nurture possibilities.

9 Little Progress No progress now. Check no undue influence from another. Practice restraint. Achieve aims later.

10 Caution Move forward boldly but with caution — success. Hesitate, others take advantage. Make amends. Show love. Ends happily.

11 Peace Little by little you succeed. Don't be rash. Reap what is sown. Plan future. Avoid secrets. Undone by deception, especially in love.

12 Obstruction Obstacles ahead, approach with determination not arrogance. Tackle challenges confidently, doors open. Holding yourself back?

13 Lovers Joining with another brings success. Emerging into light. Share benefits. New group comes into your life, opening possibilities.

14 Abundance Exceedingly fortunate time, favorable for plans. Be prepared, study, know what is required. Abundance. Good news if seeking love.

15 Modesty Have you caused offence by arrogance? Cultivate humility. Speak quietly, act gently. Someone new notices you to advantage. Be tolerant.

16 Repose Quietly contemplate all you have achieved. Sell yourself modestly but with enthusiasm. Trust feelings, leads to love.

17 Pursuit Favorable time. Go all out for what you want. Do not steamroller partners, let them reveal themselves slowly.

18 Work on What Is Spoiled Good fortune, once crisis over. Put things right or correct false impression. Apologize, but do not put your needs after others.

19 Approach Slowly No more need to push ahead assertively. Be cautious, situation may become tricky. Trust new person in your life.

20 Watchfulness Be vigilant and contemplate future. Focus on overall picture not detail. Plans may be abandoned. Challenges arise.

21 Biting Through Time to push through whatever holds you back; maybe go to law. Let go those who create problems. Ignore jealousy.

22 Grace Show true face to the world. Be elegant, but real you shines through for success. Important problem to be resolved.

23 Splitting Apart Part of life ends so new era can arise. Change of lifestyle, not separation. Do not be undermined by someone close.

24 Turning Point Successful reunion or reconciliation. Relationship improves. Right timing; change of season brings influx of energy.

25 The Unexpected Unprepared, unexpected brings problems. Do not allow temporary setbacks to throw you off balance.

26 Taking Control Unexpected good fortune arrives shortly. Take control of your life, work hard, promotion comes.

27 Watchful Waiting Time to watch and wait. Do not take too much on. Rest, regain strength, ready for action soon.

28 Excess Work within own limitations. A rival has taken on too much; step in gracefully to take over.

29 The Abyss Wait. Pitfalls ahead; you could find a worse position than now. Trust sees you through. Avoid over-involvement.

30 Shining Brightly Fortunate time for plans. Creative power is strong. Use intellect and logic not fantasy to overcome difficulties.

31 Attraction Embrace change. News of wedding fortunate omen. Good time to marry. Avoid envy.

32 Enduring Stay put. Do not make changes. Continue as you are. Acting hastily places you in worse position. Do not insist on own way.

33 Retreat Withdraw energies. Do not fight. Stay within limitations. Others may take advantage. Admit choice was wrong; take new path.

34 Strength Combine strength with gentleness to achieve aims. Proceed to success. Do not bluster. Avoid competition, especially with partner.

35 Progress Fortunes are rapidly improving. Life on up and up. Promotion likely. Keep integrity. Travel indicated.

36 Darkening Light Misery and misfortune get you down but things will improve. Do not moan. Let go painful memories. Careful planning beneficial.

37 Family Accent on family, be fair and tolerant. Family may not understand. Let woman decide. Attend to problems immediately.

38 Opposition In partnership, seek common factors. Break off unhelpful relations. Don't insist you are right.

39 Obstruction Find ways around problem — look in southwest direction. Help others with difficulties. Aid from authority figure.

40 Disentangling Situation comes to head. You know where you stand. Let go entanglements, move forward confidently.

41 Reduction Cut down on expenditure, especially energy to loved ones. Sacrifices rewarded later.

42 Increase Success due to luck rather than skill. Take advantage. Cross water for rewards. Share rewards. Give from heart.

43 Breakthrough Trouble possible. Act fast to avoid severe losses. Don't let previously good things be overtaken by bad. Avoid secrets.

44 Meeting Watch for situations or influences that entrap or weaken you. Remain calm. Do not marry.

45 Joining Together Marriage possible as love grows. Heavy expenditure beneficial. Avoid tackling opposition head on, find an ally.

46 Moving Up Progress steadily onward. Favorable for plans. Answer lies in south.

47 Adversity Hard times coming, do not run. Inner strength develops. Trust actions not words. Stay calm, all will be well.

48 The Well Miscalculation brings failure or misfortune. Don't let others take credit for your efforts. Older woman match-makes.

49 Revolution You cannot stay the same. Start again, sixth day brings success. Others find you impressive.

50 Cauldron Good omen. Confidence brings success. Attend to social life. Look after tools.

51 Thunderclaps Storms bring momentary upset. Clear the air. Light and laughter follow.

52 Stillness Keep out of way of trouble, do not be noticed. Progress slowly on chosen path. Stay calm. Avoid unnecessary gambles.

53 Progress Progress present but tiny. Marriage of young woman good omen.

54 Marrying Maiden Do not demand too much, responsibility a burden. Abandon plans. Marriage of a young woman bad omen.

55 Fullness Opportunities at their peak. Any troubles pass away. Inner calm radiates peace. Love flows.

56 The Traveler Success in small things. Travel brings rewards. Holiday prospects good. Job possibilities overseas.

57 Willing Submission Time to move up in the world. Talk to someone in authority. Reasonableness brings advancement.

58 Joy Excellent news. Things progress to your advantage. Inner spiritual harmony.

59 Dispersing Cross water to find success. Remain flexible, be reasonable. Fortunate changes in offing.

60 Restriction Work within limitations. Play by rules. Wait out difficult situations. Have something in reserve. Expand later.

61 Inner Truth Remain quietly confident. How you feel affects prospects. Difficult times may be ahead but crossing water brings luck.

62 Stay Small Not a time for huge ambition. Favors small. Conserve energy, don't panic.

63 Final Completion Do not lose through stupidity all that you gained. Things that began well could end badly. Test things out.

64 Not Yet Complete What goes wrong could turn out well. Things not finalized. Proceed cautiously, make move wisely.

Should we divorce?

Should we go to court?
Will I be successful with my suit?
Will I get alimony?

When things break apart, divorce may be the only answer. But it brings up many questions, especially concerning money and children. Astrology can give you insight into how your spouse and children react to divorce, and help you to choose an auspicious moment to go to court. Dice and the I Ching can indicate whether you should avoid going to court and playing cards can tell you whether your claims will be successful — although unless your picks match the examples, the answer may be more complicated. A very old divination method, The Egyptian Tablets, may point to the inevitability of divorce.

Sun Signs

If you want to know how either your partner or any children will react to divorce, consult the following but remember that there may be other factors in their charts that override the Sun sign and make them more vulnerable.

Aries
Male Honors financial obligations if demands reasonable. Still charges to rescue.

Female Fiercely independent but thinks she knows what's best for him.

Child Resilient, unless teenaged, when insecurity and loss of identity can set in. Defends absent parent.

Taurus
Male Pays up generously but finds it impossible to let go.

Female Loss of status hurts. Holds on. After every cent — forever.

Child Values security, takes time to adjust. Broach separation slowly.

Gemini
Male Likes to remain friends. Unreliable with alimony.

Female Independent, never clings.

Child Highly adaptable, may play one parent off against other.

Cancer
Male Pays up exactly on time but clings. Mopes.

Female Clinging martyr, extracts every cent.

Child Easily screwed up, holds emotions in, acts tough — disaster follows.

Leo

Male Generous paragon of virtue — so he says.

Female Beware her hurt pride, takes time to recover from broken heart.

Child Tough, takes over dominant role in home.

Virgo

Male Bickers over possessions, worries unduly. Pays up meticulously.

Female Criticizes, worries. May go off men.

Child Needs intellectual explanation, copes well.

Libra

Male Cannot bear discord, so pliant and generous. Remains friends.

Female Hates to bother him, may forego alimony. Soon finds another partner.

Child Always tries to please; sees both sides.

Scorpio

Male Vengeful, tries to ruin her life. Makes things difficult as possible.

Female Ditto, watch out for sting in her tail.

Child Needs truth. Penetrating insight into parents' weaknesses.

Sagittarius

Male Unreliable over finances, otherwise adaptable friend.

Female Independent, often gives up alimony. Remains loyal friend.

Child Adapts quickly when given space.

Capricorn

Male Pays on time. Prone to depression.

Female May turn into money-grabbing depressive.

Child Natural survivor, prone to gloom.

Aquarius

Male Elusive, detached, kiss goodbye to alimony.

Female Quickly forgets why divorced.

Child Emotionally detached; needs full explanation then gets on with life.

Pisces

Male Legal knot broken, emotional one isn't. Erratic but generous with alimony.

Female Sucker, still involved at an emotional level.

Child Dependent, needs oodles of love and reassurance. Avoid guilt.

Dice

There may be certain things that you do not really want to come out in public. If you have any concerns about this and roll seven from a pair of dice, you may want to think twice about going to court.

 Seven You could be involved in a scandal.

Playing Cards

The cards can indicate whether a good alimony settlement is coming your way. Shuffle the pack, cut and turn up the top card:

> ***Nine of Clubs*** Large alimony settlement.
>
> ***Ace or King of Spades*** Lawsuit, lawyer and judge.

I Ching

The Chinese always consulted the *I Ching* before going to law. To consult this great oracle, you must create a hexagram (six-line figure) by throwing three coins six times. Each time you throw a majority of heads, you draw an unbroken line and each time the majority is tails, you sketch a broken line. Start at the bottom and build up. Compare your hexagram with the one below. If you ask about divorcing, you could have no better omen than:

 21 Biting Through Legal matters are successful.

See pages 66–69 for explanations of other hexagrams.

Palmistry

Again, your hand is a good indication of what will happen. It may show that you reconcile or divorce or that your partner will make life difficult for you.

Reconciliation
If you hope your lover will come back, look at your Marriage Lines. If a break in one line is bridged by a line beneath, there is every chance of a reconciliation.

Divorce
If a Marriage Line frays at the end, separation is indicated. If your Heart Line has a distinct break, with frayed ends, and a new line starts off, divorce is probable.

Egyptian Tablets

If you question these ancient stones about parting, deception, money, or going to law, look out for numbers below. Consult the tablets overleaf to learn more.

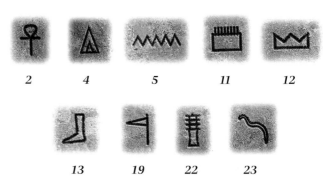

| 2 | 4 | 5 | 11 | 12 |

| 13 | 19 | 22 | 23 |

Egyptian Tablets

The ancient Egyptians had many forms of divination. To them, the gods had a hand in everything. Fortune could be bought with offerings, an outcome predicted by signs from on high. While random chance appears to determine the outcome when using the Tablets, their originators would say that the wise god, Thoth, guided your hand.

Method

Using a pencil or a pin, pierce one of the hieroglyphs overleaf at random.
Consult the key to see to which number the hieroglyph corresponds.

Find your answer on page 75.

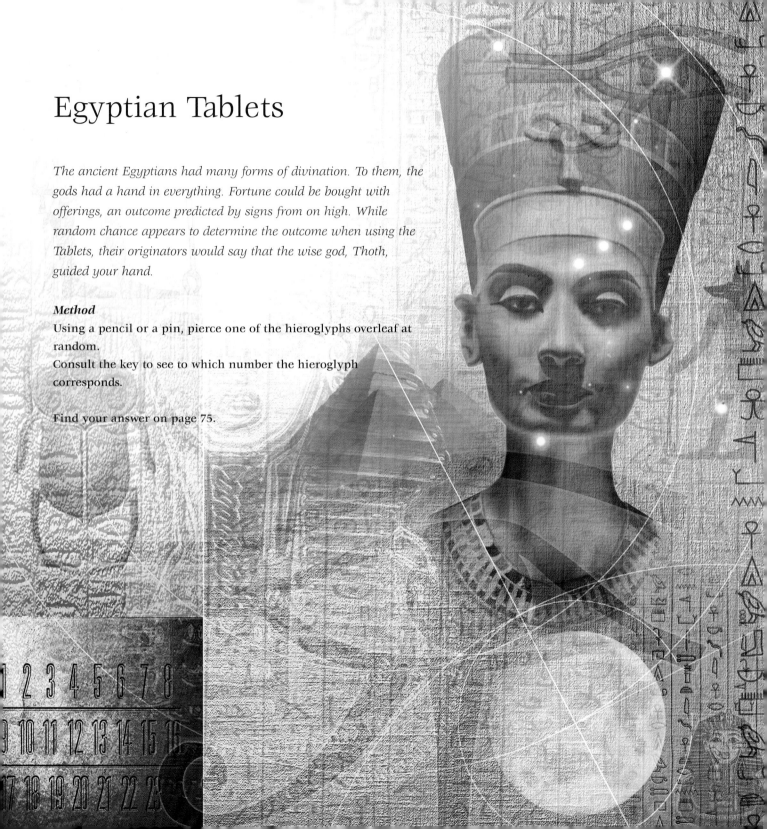

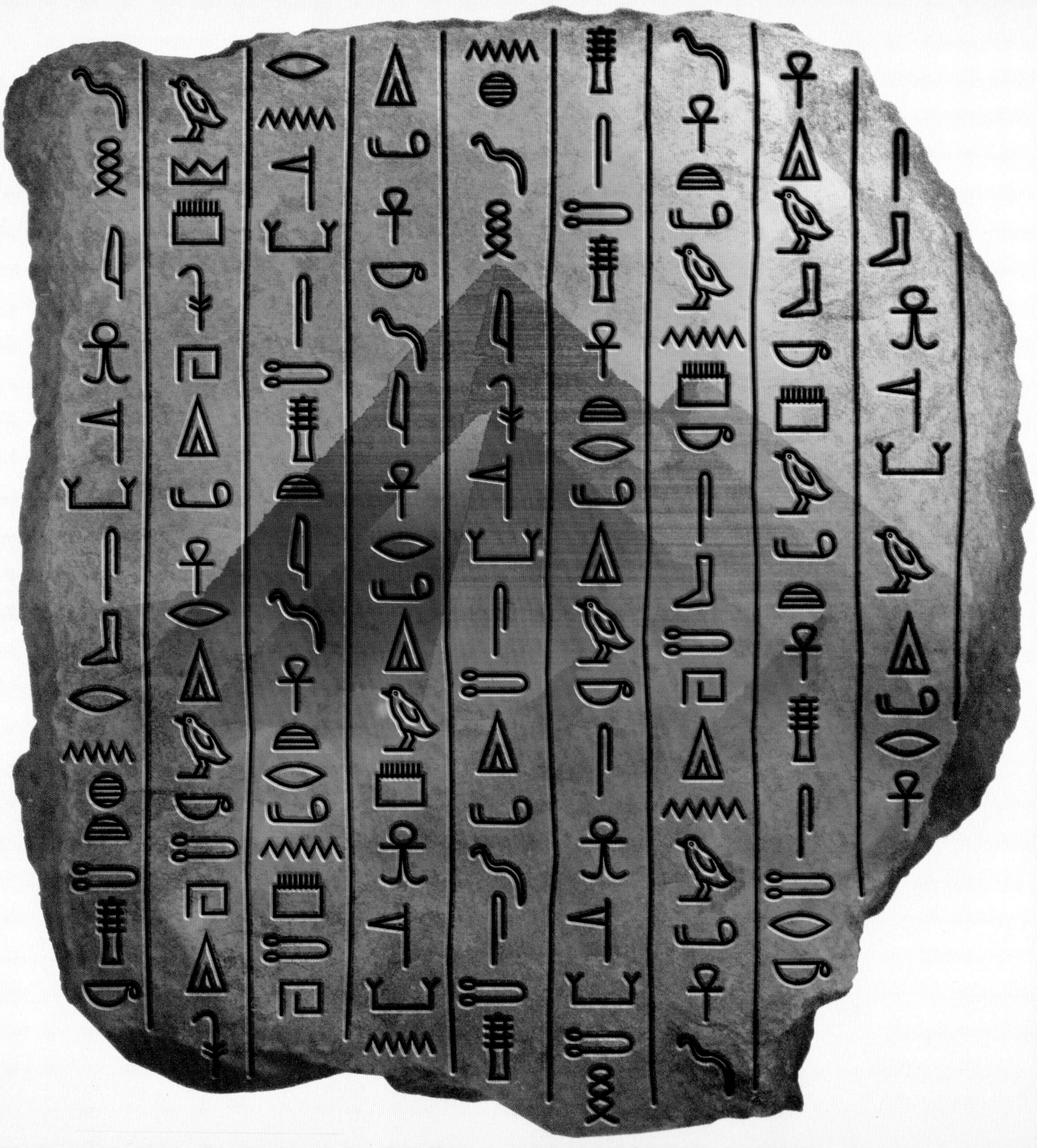

1 For a single man, a wife homely but rich. For a single woman, faithfulness in your lover and speedy marriage.

2 Loss of a friend or money, unfaithfulness of lover, unsatisfactory partner, failure at law.

3 Excellent fortune, sudden prosperity, respect from superiors, letter containing important news.

4 Letter announcing loss of money or status.

5 Divorce or parting of the ways.

6 Undertakings will fail.

7 If single, a handsome, rich and faithful husband. If married, a partner of good family, you married above your station.

8 Expectations will be fulfilled and undertakings prosper.

9 If married and under 50, a child is likely. If single, sudden marriage.

10 Friend or colleague returns from overseas bringing shared prosperity.

11 Fidelity of husband or wife is questionable. If single, you are shockingly deceived.

12 Success in all your undertakings.

13 Hopes of borrowing money will come to nothing. Beware deception.

14 The older man on whom you depend will marry and have a child.

15 Although you have not yet made your mark, if well-intentioned friends assist, you find good fortune and eminence.

16 Sudden journey with congenial companion results in good fortune, especially to family.

17 In present company, you pretend to sneer at oracles, but secretly rely on them, and yet will be disgraced.

18 Sudden acquaintance with the opposite sex brings opposition. Persevere; ultimately it will be to your advantage.

19 Beware of those who owe you money, even if a little. Letter of abuse can be expected.

20 A partner who drinks too much. Poor success in business but you will never be penniless, although you will not be happy.

21 An important letter will arrive, announcing the death of someone you had little respect for but who has left you a legacy.

22 A precarious number. Your conduct will determine outcome. Be prudent and future will be good.

23 An unlucky number. Behave well. Justice, though slow, overtakes the ill-intentioned or devious person.

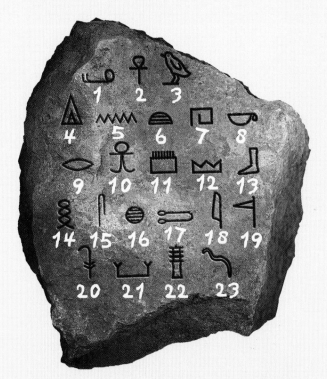

Family
and
Home

16

Family and home are close to everyone's heart. They provide your basic security in life, your deep rooted experiences, and a place from which to venture confidently out into the world. A supportive family life makes you much more adventurous and enables you to feel positive about the future.

After investigating romance, most people start to question matters involving their families and homes. If they are married, they want to know when would be a good time to start a family or they seek help in understanding their children and what the future holds for them. They may be considering moving house and want to know whether this is a good time to make a move and, if so, in what direction.

As in all matters pertaining to timing, there are many ways to answer these questions. Life has a natural rhythm, an ebb and flow of energies. There are times when conception and birth are powerful forces and the urge to procreate strong. However, biological pressures do not always result in children. This is why phrasing your question is so important. Simply asking about having a baby might bring the answer "yes" but the "baby" in question turns out to be a new pet or the completion of a novel.

Creativity is not always biological. You may be giving birth to a new part of yourself, to a creative project, a new start in life, or a different way of living as a family. The same can apply to moving. If you ask "When will I move?" and the answer indicates next week, it could indicate a major shift taking place within you rather than a physical move. If all your energy is focused on the outer move, you could well miss the opportunity that the inner shift brings — and believe that the oracle was wrong.

Is now the right time to start a family?

When will I have a baby?

How many children will I have?

A frequently asked divinatory question is: "Will I have a child?" People also want to know when, what sex and, ultimately, how many. Dice can provide a quick answer. If people are having difficulty conceiving they want to know why this is and if it will pass; Astrology can be helpful here. Fortunate Days can help you use your birthday to find a good time to conceive and work with positive energies to bring about desired results. Finally, the ancient art of Geomancy has been used to answer fertility questions for generations.

Dice

Rolling a pair of dice on or shortly after your wedding day provides yes or no answers as to whether you will soon have a child. If you do not receive a positive answer, don't worry, it will probably take a little longer. For the full meaning of the dice, see page 161.

 Six and Four Yes!

Western Astrology

The fifth house is the house of both creativity and children. If Jupiter is in this house in your birthchart, you will probably have a large family. When Jupiter moves through the bottom of your chart it signifies a time of conception or increased creativity.

If you are having difficulty conceiving and know your birthchart, look to see whether Saturn is placed in your fifth house. This planet indicates delays or difficulties and could mean that your life plan is to have children later in life, or not at all.

If you do not know your birthchart, counting your Sun sign as number 1, count forward counterclockwise four more signs to find the fifth house, the House of Creativity. Consult the Astrological Tables (see pages 185–8) to find out if Jupiter or Saturn is passing through.

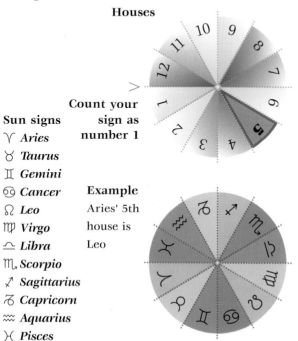

Houses

Count your sign as number 1

Sun signs

♈ *Aries*
♉ *Taurus*
♊ *Gemini*
♋ *Cancer*
♌ *Leo*
♍ *Virgo*
♎ *Libra*
♏ *Scorpio*
♐ *Sagittarius*
♑ *Capricorn*
♒ *Aquarius*
♓ *Pisces*

Example
Aries' 5th house is Leo

Fortunate Days

It may take a bit of time and careful planning but using a combination of your Birthdate Number (found by adding all the separate digits of your full date of birth), the day of the week, and the number for the current date (found by adding the digits of the date), you can pinpoint a propitious day to try for a baby. The easiest way to do this is to take each possible date in the middle of your cycle, calculate its number and determine the day it falls on. Then look it up under your Birthdate Number (see page 139). If your Birthdate Number is 5, the date number 3, and the day Saturday, love could well lead to a family. If your Birthdate Number is 7, the day number 1 and the day Wednesday, pregnancy could have you changing your plans!

Geomancy

Geomancy divines answers from random marks made on paper. To ask whether you should try for a baby now, you need to create a geomantic figure. Make four lines of random dashes across a piece of paper one below the other (**do not count as you go**). Add up the number of dashes in each line. At the end of each odd-numbered line, put a large dot •. At the end of each even-numbered line, put two large dots ••. Overleaf you will find the 16 possible figures you can create — and their meanings.

If you drew the following example: an odd-numbered line followed by two even-numbered lines followed by an odd-numbered line, the resultant figure would be

 Carcer An indication of pregnancy.

If you want to work with the full geomantic chart (see overleaf), then Carcer falling in your fifth house would be most fortuitous.

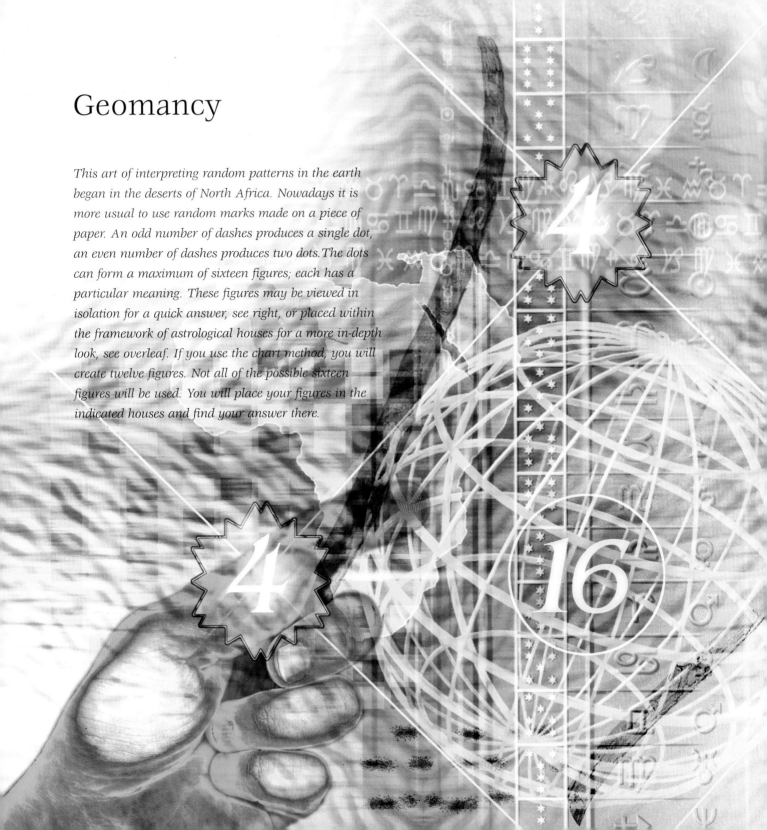

Geomancy

This art of interpreting random patterns in the earth began in the deserts of North Africa. Nowadays it is more usual to use random marks made on a piece of paper. An odd number of dashes produces a single dot, an even number of dashes produces two dots. The dots can form a maximum of sixteen figures; each has a particular meaning. These figures may be viewed in isolation for a quick answer, see right, or placed within the framework of astrological houses for a more in-depth look, see overleaf. If you use the chart method, you will create twelve figures. Not all of the possible sixteen figures will be used. You will place your figures in the indicated houses and find your answer there.

Puer A boy, yellow and beardless. Male principle. Decisive action: foolish or wise. Events heralding growth. Fortunate in competitive situations. Exciting love affair.

Amissio Material loss. Divorce — no alimony. Unprofitable deal or investment. Deceit and trickery. Faulty purchase. Good fortune in love.

Albus White-haired one. Sagacity, clarity, practicality. Authority. Good fortune. Communication. Fresh start: new job, house move. Freedom from past restrictions.

Via Way or road. Stay on the chosen path. Fortunate for journeys and solo enterprises but not joint ventures. Shows way through present difficulties.

Populus Favors group and social activities. May indicate a wedding. Community projects. Do not go it alone or start new solo projects.

Fortuna Major Greater fortune. Commercial success. Interior and exterior aid. Worldly ambitions fulfilled. Increased wealth or status. Long-term projects well aspected. Good luck.

Fortuna Minor Good fortune, success. Successful outcome to longstanding matters, especially legal proceedings. Completion.

Conjunctio Coming together, joining. Marriage, close ties of all kinds. Cements existing relationships. New alliances highly rewarding: personal or business.

Puella Beautiful, charming young woman. Female principle. Fiery passion. New romance. Greater understanding. Excellent for children's affairs, domestic issues, partnerships.

Rubeus Red headed. Passion, fiery temper. Force and power, destruction. Do not allow strong emotions to overrule good sense. Disgrace, injustice, scandal.

Acquisitio Acquisition. Success, gain, expansion. Worldly achievements. Travel, actual and mental. Improvement in status. Financial backing forthcoming.

Carcer Delays, obstacles, restrictions. Changes in plans. Missed opportunities. Pregnancy, new concepts. Fortunate for birth.

Tristitia Sadness, grief, heaviness. Despair and despondency. Retrenchment in business. Loss of position. Plans fail. Debauchery.

Laetitia Good fortune, joy, laughter. Good health. End of doubts or difficult circumstances. Recovery from illness. Favorable legal judgment. Celebration.

Caput Draconis The inner threshold. Good fortune. Unexpected developments for the better. Travel. Emigration/work overseas.

Cauda Draconis The outer threshold. Favorable for all matters of the heart. Can be harbinger of disaster. Requires persistence and good intent.

Geomantic chart

Make sixteen rows of random dashes one below the
other. Add up the number of dashes in each line.
Odd number: place one large dot at the end of the row.
Even number: place two large dots at the end of the row.
Each set of four lines of dots forms a geomantic figure;
the first four figures are known as "the Mothers."

To form Figure 5, use the first lines of Figures 1–4.
Example

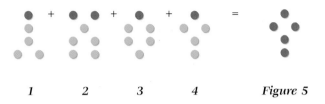

| 1 | 2 | 3 | 4 | Figure 5 |

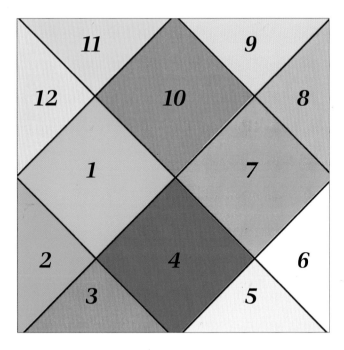

To form Figure 6, use the second lines of Figures 1–4;
To form Figure 7, use the third lines of Figures 1–4;
To form Figure 8, use the fourth lines of Figures 1–4.
For the last four figures, 9–12, you will have to add two
figures together. Where the lines produce an odd
number, put one dot and where they combine to make
an even number, add two dots:

• + •• = •; • + • = ••.

To form Figure 9, add Figures 1 and 2 together.
To form Figure 10, add Figures 3 and 4 together.
To form Figure 11, add figures 5 and 6 together.
To form Figure 12, add figures 7 and 8 together.
Place Figure 1 in the tenth house on the Chart, figure 2
in the first house, figure 3 in the fourth house, figure 4
in the seventh house, figure 5 in the eleventh house,
figure 6 in the second house, figure 7 in the fifth house,
figure 8 in the eighth house, figure 9 in the twelfth
house, figure 10 in the third house, figure 11 in the sixth
house and figure 12 in the ninth house.

1 *Vitality, Life, Health, Enquiries*
2 *Money, Property, Personal Worth, Possessions*
3 *Siblings, Communications, Short Journeys, News*
4 *Parents, Inheritance, The End of the Matter*
5 *Love, Children, Pleasure, Speculation, Creativity*
6 *Employees, Health, Relations, Small Animals*
7 *Marriage, Partner, Contracts, Public Enemies,
   Lawsuits*
8 *Death, Legacies, Pain*
9 *Long Journeys, Science, Visions, Art*
10 *Parents, Trade or Profession, Honor and Rank*
11 *Friends, Hopes, Community, Wishes*
12 *Sorrows, Fears, Institutions, Unseen Danger, Secret
   Enemies*

Will it be a boy or a girl?

Many people want to know the sex of a prospective child. Palmistry can tell you whether you will have a girl or a boy, and how many children you will have in all. Dowsing is another quick way to determine the sex of your child.

Palmistry

Lines on your hand can indicate whether your child will be a boy or a girl. A thick vertical line at the bottom of your little finger toward the outer edge indicates a boy, a thin line a girl.

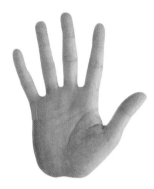 

A thick line for a boy   *A thin line for a girl*

Pendulum dowsing

A traditional way to tell whether you will have a boy or girl is to suspend a wedding ring tied to a ribbon or cord over your pregnant stomach. Refer to page 137 to see how to hold the "pendulum." If the ring swings clockwise, it will be a boy. If it swings counterclockwise, it will be a girl.

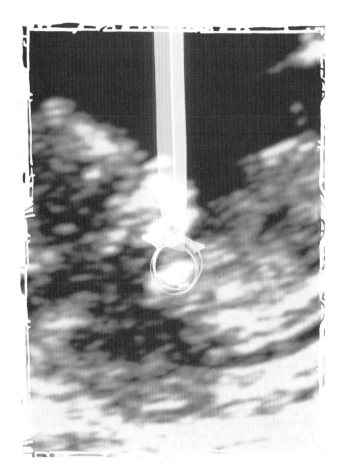

What kind of person is my child?

What will my child be like?
Is my child happy or unhappy?
Will she be beautiful?
What are his/her traits?

There are many systems of divination that will help you to know your child's potential, and his or her Sun sign, for example, can give you enormous insight. While it can be very exciting to see a child's potential, the danger is that you will push your child toward it and not allow your child to develop in as well rounded a way as possible. You can encourage a child to bring out innate talents, but do not block progress by being too fixed in your own agenda. It is always worth remembering that potential is just that: a possibility. Being as flexible as possible will enable your child to grow in the best possible way. However, should your child experience problems, The Hand of Fatima, can help you discern the reasons.

Sun Signs

Knowing your child's Sun sign gives you a starting point for assessing your child's strengths and weaknesses, and into areas of conflict and harmony within the family. Bear in mind, however, that other factors in a natal birthchart could well modify the Sun sign.

The Aries Child Independent, "me" orientated, assertive, energetic. Believes s/he is right. Hot tempered. Strong willed, impetuous, frank. Very competitive, always on the go. All or nothing person. Bossy. Affectionate. Pioneering initiator, starts well but doesn't finish. Courageous, no fear. Go-getter; takes the world by storm.

The Taurus Child Conservative, likes security, dependable, persistent. Stubborn. Hates routine disrupted. Slow fuse, powerful temper. Musical, artistic, practical and mechanically skilled. Never gives up, yet can be lazy. Plodder, will not be rushed. Loyal and loving. Enjoys cuddles — and food. May have weight problem. Shapes the world.

The Gemini Child Talkative, communicative, creative, playful. Live wire, rarely sits still. Curious and inventive. Runs on nervous energy, mentally over-active, talks in sleep. Short concentration span. Multi-tasks. Mischievous, impish sense of humor. Two people in one; changeable. Lies. Independent, dislikes cuddles. Comments on the world.

The Cancer Child Emotional, home-loving, moody. Highly sensitive and insecure. Easily hurt; prone to self-pity. Tenacious, possessive — especially of mother. Imaginative and caring. Quiet. Oblique, approaches things sideways on. Money-orientated. Clinging, demands cuddles. Hidden ambition. Nurtures the world.

The Leo Child Dramatic, sunny, loving, playful. A delight — or a tyrant. Demands his/her own way. Highly creative. Dresses up, loves to perform. Adores flattery. Craves an audience. Many friends — who are dominated. Strong pride. Likes routine. Highly affectionate and doesn't hesitate to show it. Wants to rule the world.

The Virgo Child Precise, observant, obedient, shy. Intellectual and practical. Tidy, enjoys routine. Well-behaved. The only child who stays clean. Cool. Unemotional but can get upset over small things. Picky about food. Fussy about health. Self critical — seeks impossible perfection. Needs to set realistic goals. Serves the world.

The Libra Child Charming, artistic, flirtatious, friendly. Wants to please, needs relationships. Indecisive. Laid back. Dislikes upset. Tactful, lies to save hurting others. Cannot say no. Likes animals. Sensual, affectionate, needs cuddles. Seeks justice and fairness. Harmonizes the world.

The Scorpio Child Secretive, intense, unfathomable. Strong willed. Ruthless. Loyal. Enjoys solitude. Powerful imagination. Perceptive and insightful. Intensely jealous and possessive. Needs security and routine. Strong temper, can be destructive. Holds grudges forever. Seeks to master the world.

The Sagittarius Child Independent, uninhibited, active, freedom loving, needs space. Curious, natural explorer, no fear. Spontaneous, careless, lacks discipline and boundaries. Talkative, frank, friendly. Always questioning, wants to know. Sporty or uncoordinated. Tactless. Poor liar. Enjoys being educated. Dislikes cuddles.

The Capricorn Child Self-contained, cautious, serious. Late developer. Works hard, obeys rules, likes boundaries, Strong sense of responsibility. Pessimistic, offset by keen sense of humor. Enjoys history and tradition. Ambitious, seeks social status even in childhood. Money-orientated. Wants to be top of the world.

The Aquarius Child Rebellious, independent, unpredictable seeker of truth. Non-conformer. Broad minded, future-orientated, experimenter. Drawn to science, the unusual, bizarre, and weird. Sets trends. Oblivious to time. Emotionally detached, dislikes cuddles. Empathy with social, charitable and ecological concerns. Could save the world.

The Pisces Child Dreamy, artistic, fantasy-orientated. Easily influenced. Confuses make-believe and reality. Dislikes responsibility. Needs boundaries. Emotionally expressive, seeks comfort and cuddles. Sympathetic. Non-competitive. Prone to over-indulgence. Play-acting becomes real. Wants to make the world one.

The Hand of Fatima

Most people name their child without giving thought to the qualities it imparts. The Hand of Fatima (see page 30) can throw light on such matters. It can help you to understand your child or to pinpoint underlying problems such as why s/he is unhappy.

Follow the instructions for obtaining your child's individual number. If it is 17 and s/he is having problems at school, then inability to concentrate could be the cause. 18 would indicate that stubbornness was at the root of problems, while the victim mentality under-lying 1095 could well attract bullying, as could 34. A child with number 6 could well find that perfectionism led to setting too high a goal to be sensibly reached but a child with number 5 is headed toward happiness, wealth, and a happy marriage.

Inappropriate questions

Some people become hooked on oracles, not making a move without consulting their favorite prognosticator. The danger in relying too heavily on oracles is that you then get the answer you want rather than what will really occur. You can also try to make something happen, and thus block other possibilities, but you may have misinterpreted the answer, or asked an inappropriate question in the first place. There are some questions that it is inappropriate to ask an oracle. "Is my child skipping school?" is an example. The sensible thing to do is to ask the school!

How will we get along?

Why are we always arguing?

Why don't we understand each other?

Finding out how compatible you are with your child can be very useful if you're not getting along. It can help you to see your child more as an individual and enjoy your differences rather than fight against them.

Sun Signs

To know how you will get along with your child, refer to the chart below to compare your sign and your child's.

- **•** Easy, no friction
- **••** Easy, "good friends"
- **•••** Easy, "mutual admiration"
- **•••** Same basic outlook but some conflicts
- **•••** Well balanced, some arguments
- **•••** Challenges; dissimilar people or too alike
- **•••** Little point of contact
- **•••** Difficult, each wants own way
- **•••** Total opposites

	♈	♉	♊	♋	♌	♍	♎	♏	♐	♑	♒	♓
♈ **Aries**	•••	••••	••	•••	•••	•••	•••	•••	•••	•••	••	•••
♉ **Taurus**	••••	•••	•••	••	•••	•••	•••	•••	••••	•••	•••	•
♊ **Gemini**	••	••••	•••	•••	••	•••	•••	•••	•••	•••	•••	•••
♋ **Cancer**	•••	•	•••	•••	•••	••	•••	•••	•••	•••	•••	•••
♌ **Leo**	••	••••	•••	•••	•••	•••	•••	•••	•••	••••	•••	•••
♍ **Virgo**	•••	•••	•••	•••	•••	•••	•••	••	•••	•••	•••	•••
♎ **Libra**	••	•••	•••	•••	•••	•••	•••	••••	•••	•••	•••	•••
♏ **Scorpio**	•••	•••	•••	•••	•••	•••	••••	•••	••••	•	•••	•••
♐ **Sagittarius**	•••	••••	•••	•••	•••	•••	••	•••	•••	••••	•••	•••
♑ **Capricorn**	•••	•••	•••	•••	•••	•••	•••	••	•••	•••	•••	•••
♒ **Aquarius**	•••	•••	•••	•••	•••	•••	••	•••	••	•••	•••	•••
♓ **Pisces**	•••	••	•••	••	•••	•••	•••	•••	•••	•••	•••	•••

Western Astrology

A combination of fate and freewill, astrology says that the time you were born is significant because it tells you a great deal about yourself and what you are meant to be — that is, it is a picture of your fate — and it gives you opportunities to move beyond into your destiny and be all that you can be.

The Zodiac is divided into twelve signs through which the Sun passes during a year — giving rise to Sun sign astrology. The signs are the background against which the energies of planets manifest. Planets move at varying speeds around the Zodiac, some taking a month (the Moon), others taking several human lifetimes (Neptune and Pluto). When the Zodiac is translated into a birthchart, it has divisions, called Houses, which the planets inhabit. It is the relationship these planets make to each other, and the signs in which they sit, which reflect your innate qualities. How the planets progress from there affects your future.

A birthchart is a "frozen" moment in time. It shows how you will most probably behave, how you will react to challenges, your expectations and ingrained patterns of behavior, whether you will be an extrovert or an introvert and the kind of interests you will have. A birth chart, however, is not static; it moves and changes as the planets pass overhead. These movements, called transits, trigger potentials and possibilities.

What you must be

It has been said that a birthchart is a seed. The seed may be for an apple or a rose, but an apple cannot become a rose. It can become, however, the biggest and most beautiful apple in the world. In other words, a seed can fulfill its potential to the highest point. If a seed is well nurtured, growing in good soil with light and sunshine, it will develop well. If it is starved, grown in the dark without light, then it will be a stunted apple. People are exactly the same. If a child is encouraged to be his or her own natural self, that child will flourish. The child may be destined to be an apple or a rose. But whichever he or she becomes, there will be trigger moments throughout life that help growth to reach full potential.

Freewill and astrology

Where freewill comes into astrology is through those trigger moments; freewill grasps them, makes necessary changes and grows into the fullness of being — whether it be apple or rose. Someone who follows a fatalistic view of life looks on those trigger moments as something from outside, something done to them over which they have no control. But with freewill, they become opportunities to take control.

The Birthchart

A birthchart is calculated for the date, place, and time you were born. The birthchart opposite is that for this book. (It is for my first contact with the publisher, but it would also be possible to look at the publication date.) I have always looked on my books as "children," something I give birth to. The chart has a metaphysical Scorpio Ascendant (the face it presents to the world) and an analytical Virgo Midheaven (what is strived for). Far-sighted Aquarius is the communicative Third House and the planet that represents the mind, Mercury, is in the occult Eighth House. Master of all that, Pluto, is hidden in the questing sign of Sagittarius in the First House. Perfect for a book that seeks to penetrate and explain the mysteries of the future! The Sun is in Leo in

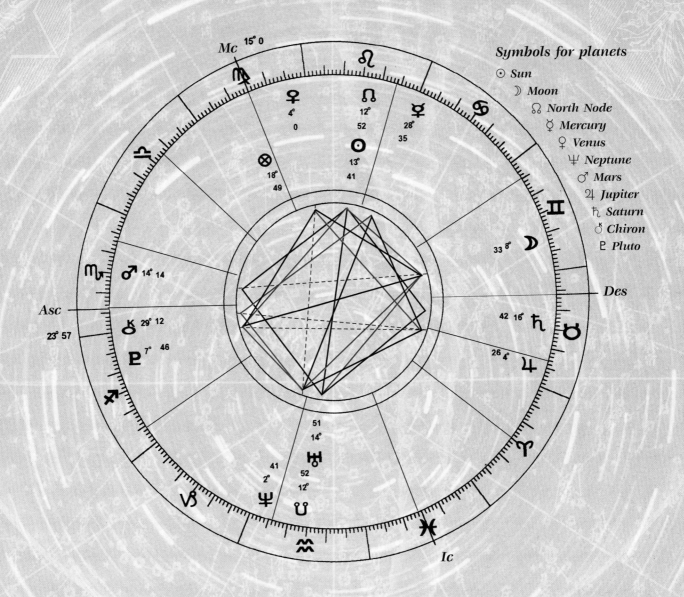

Mc 15° 0

Symbols for planets

☉ Sun
☽ Moon
☊ North Node
☿ Mercury
♀ Venus
♆ Neptune
♂ Mars
♃ Jupiter
♄ Saturn
⚷ Chiron
♇ Pluto

♃ 4°
12° 0

☊
12° 52

♀ ♍
0

☿
28° 35

☉
13°
41

⊗
18°
49

33 8° ☽

Des

Asc

♂ 14° 14

42 16° ♄

23° 57

⚷ 29° 12

26 4° ♃

♇ 7° 46

51
14°

41
2°

♅
52
12°

♆ ☊

Ic

The signs (Outer ring) The position of the signs differs according to the time you were born.

The ascendant (Asc) The sign coming over the horizon when you were born.

The planets (Middle ring) The placement of the planets differs according to the time you were born.

The houses (Segments of middle ring) This chart uses the Placidus House method, Equal House would give a slightly different structure.

The aspects (Center) The geometric relationship between the planets at your birth.

Western Astrology | 89

the Ninth House of Publishing. The idea has plenty of drive and energy behind it, especially with the expansive planet of success, Jupiter, lending a hand in the Fifth House of Creativity. Visionary Neptune with its ability to pierce the veil is a personal resource I bring to the writing of the book (the Second House) while Mercury in Cancer is the nurturing care given to it by the publisher. The book looks to have a great future!

The Houses
Astrology has several systems of House division. The "quick" method used in this book employs Equal House as this does not need complicated calculations. It gives you a background against which the moving planets can be placed. There are other methods, the technicalities of which need not concern us here, and the example chart uses another system, Placidus. Each House relates to a sphere of life:

First House Individuality and coming into incarnation.
Second House Personal resources and values.
Third House Communication, short journeys, siblings.
Fourth House Family and roots.
Fifth House Creativity, love affairs, children.
Sixth House Health and vocation.
Seventh House Partnerships and marriage.
Eighth House Inheritance and shared resources, metaphysics, death, and rebirth.
Ninth House Philosophy, education, and long journeys.
Tenth House Family, work, and outer environment.
Eleventh House Groups, hopes, wishes.
Twelfth House What is hidden.

Planets and signs
Planets activate and energize. When they are moving through signs they act through the lens of that sign, taking on its qualities. Planets can be said to function:

Impetuously and ardently in *Aries*
Productively and concretely in *Taurus*
Persuasively and diversely in *Gemini*
Protectively and circuitously in *Cancer*
Ebulliently and powerfully in *Leo*
Discerningly and logically in *Virgo*
Cooperatively and equably in *Libra*
Perspicaciously and intensely in *Scorpio*
Inquiringly and enthusiastically in *Sagittarius*
Authoritatively and conservatively in *Capricorn*
Objectively and far-sightedly in *Aquarius*
Amorphously and imaginatively in *Pisces*

Progressed Charts
As charts are not fixed and static, astrologers use something called progression to see how your life is panning out and what new influences are coming into play, but this is beyond the scope of this book.

Transits
As the planets move overhead, they affect the planets in your natal chart. Transits have been used through this book to give you fast insight into timing and opportunities. (More detail is given when an astrologer reads your chart.)

Sun Sign Astrology

While your birth chart is a picture of a unique person — you — the signs have a tendency to behave in certain ways and a specific personality type and certain characteristics are attributed to each. Aries is impetuous, for example, Capricorn cautious. Other factors in your chart may mask these tendencies, or strengthen them, but the underlying attributes will be there. These tendencies may well be brought to the surface when a planet passes through your Sun sign, seemingly triggering emotions or events in your external life that actually have a great deal to do with your inner life and the way you manifest these attributes in your world.

Aries
March 21–April 20
Initiative, courage, impulse, enterprise, thrust, passion, leadership, egotism.

Cancer
June 22–July 23
Emotionality, sympathy, nurture, defensiveness, vulnerability, clingingness, tenacity, ambition.

Libra
September 24–October 23
Relatedness, partnership, cooperation, diplomacy, conciliation, indecisiveness, compromise, judgment.

Capricorn
December 22–January 20
Authority, discipline, conservation, caution, responsibility, consistency, scapegoat, society.

Taurus
April 21–May 21
Endurance, steadfastness, productivity, practicality, security, fixity, sensuality, stubbornness.

Leo
July 24–August 23
Regality, pride, enthusiasm, drama, self-assurance, generosity, opinionated-ness, playfulness.

Scorpio
October 24–November 22
Intensity, mastery, magnetism, penetration, power, sexuality, secrets, transformation.

Aquarius
January 21–February 19
Detachment, revolution, reason, eccentricity, idealism, brotherhood, foresight.

Gemini
May 22–June 21
Multifacetedness, adaptability, duality, duplicity, versatility, inquisitiveness, sociability, superficiality.

Virgo
August 24–September 23
Discrimination, analysis, critique, efficiency, perfectionism, service, purity, fruitfulness.

Sagittarius
November 23–December 21
Quest, questioning, adventure, spontaneity, optimism, tactlessness, philosophy, freedom.

Pisces
February 20–March 20
Compassion, mysticism, impressionability, receptivity, vacillation, imagination, malleability, transcendent.

The Zodiac Wheel

A flowing band of interweaving energies, the Zodiac Wheel takes a little getting used to as it is read anti-clockwise starting at Aries, where 9 o'clock would be on a clockface.

The outer band of the wheel shows the symbols traditionally associated with each sign. Aries is the Ram, for instance, Taurus the bull. Signs are said to have characteristics of their symbols. Libra, for instance, weighs things up just like its symbol, the Scales.

Each sign belongs to what is known as an element, shown in the third band. There are four elements: fire, earth, air, and water. Each element has three signs belonging to it. Signs belonging to each element share certain characteristics and describe how people go out to meet the world. So, if you have the Sun in fire (Aries, Leo, and Sagittarius), you will be fiery and outgoing, positive and impetuous. With the Sun in practical Earth (Taurus, Virgo, and Capricorn), you will be much more restrained. Earth signs are concerned with security and with careful planning. Air signs are cerebral, quick, communicative, and innovative. Fluid water signs (Cancer, Scorpio, and Pisces) are emotional and feeling orientated.

The fourth band shows whether a sign is cardinal, fixed, or mutable. There is one fire sign that is cardinal: Aries, one that is fixed: Leo, and one that is mutable: Sagittarius, and so on. The qualities describe how the energies flow in a person.

Cardinal signs are active, enterprising, and outgoing, enjoying a challenge. The cardinal sign of each element is the most forceful, relatively speaking. So, Capricorn, who is cardinal, is the most authoritative and enterprising of the Earth signs, although still cautious in accordance with its earth nature. The fixed signs are exactly what their name suggests: rigid, resistant to change and fond of routines. Steadfast Taurus, who is fixed, is the most entrenched Earth sign. Mutable signs enjoy change, they are flexible and adaptable. Virgo, who is the flexible earth sign, has its natural resistance to change broken down by the mutable element.

Signs also are what is known as "positive" or "negative." This is not a judgmental term. Positive means active and outgoing, negative signs are passive and reflective. Because of the way the signs are organized, Fire and Air signs are positive, and Earth and Water signs are negative.

All birthcharts are a complex interweaving sea of energies. Some will have many planets in cardinal signs, which can overcome a passive Sun sign. Others may be mutable and negative, holding back a usually enterprising Sun sign. This is why the individual birthchart is so important.

The Zodiac key

Fire   *Cardinal*

Earth   *Fixed*

Water   *Mutable*

Air

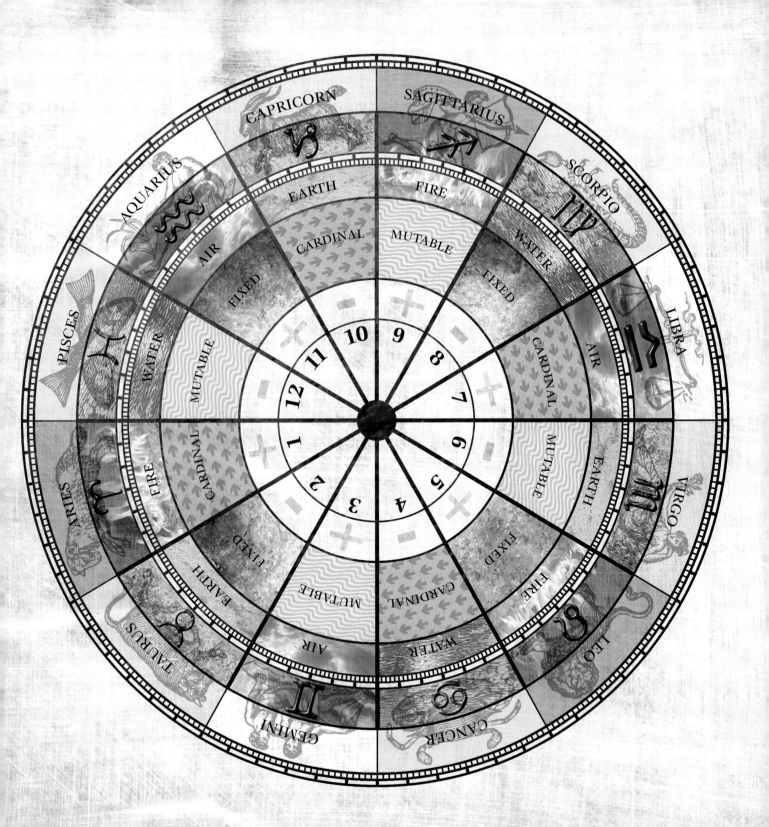

What is going on in my family?

Does my family think of me often?

Will my parents support me in what I want to do?

Are family members hiding something from me?

Concerns often arise when you have been separated from your family for a while. You may have a secret you haven't shared with them — Dominoes may be able to supply the reassurance you need. You may feel family members are keeping something from you. The Egyptian Tablets, The Square of 36, and The Wheel of Destiny can be used to find if this is so — and what it is.

Egyptian Tablets

These are particularly good at pinpointing matters that are being hidden from you, so use this technique to find out if your family is practicing a deception. Turn to the tablets on page 74. Mark one of the hieroglyphs at random. Consult the key to see to which number it corresponds. Some answers may seem obscure but many are self-evident including those picked out below:

 4 Could well indicate redundancy or losses on the stock market.

 5 A parting of the ways is being considered.

 11 Infidelity or some other deception may be causing problems.

 20 A problem with alcohol may be being covered up.

The Square of 36

Playing cards can ascertain whether you are being deceived by your family and what the result could be. Shuffle a pack and deal into six rows of six as shown. Look at the card in position 20 (Deception).

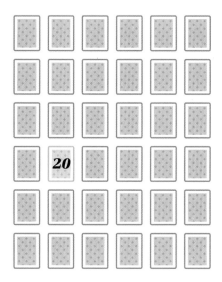

♥ **Hearts** Someone in the family could be scheming against you, but the scheme will backfire.

♠ **Spades** Bring things out into the open or your reputation could be adversely affected.

♦ **Diamonds** Remain calm, whatever it is has little significance and will quickly pass.

♣ **Clubs** If you suspect there is something going on, talk things over with a trusted family member.

Wheel of Destiny

This can help you to understand what is going on in your family and how it might affect you. Turn to page 132 and put your finger underneath the Family section. With your eyes closed, stick a pin at random above your finger. Then read off the answers.

1, **2**, and **3** There may be financial schemes afoot.

4 Dysfunctional patterns you learned from your family are holding you back. Some therapy could release you.

6 A death is indicated but this is not always to be taken literally in divination; something may be ending rather than a person dying. But if someone is moving out of the family, now is the time to say everything that needs to be said and to tie up loose ends so that there are no future regrets.

Dominoes

If you need to know whether your family will support you, try asking the dominoes. Place them face down on a table. Concentrate on your question, swirl them around and then pick one at random:

 Double Six Helpful and supportive parents.

Double One Parents will be particularly helpful if a decision requires courage.

 Four-Two A family upheaval. The answer could be the opposite of what you expect.

 Three-Blank Weakness or jealousy in family members could mean lack of support.

Is this a good time to move?

Is this an auspicious time to sell?

When to move is a major concern. A quick answer may be supplied by Runes, while Numerology can give you insight into what stage you are in your Life Cycle. Numerology is not static and fixed. It deals with unfolding nine-year cycles that exercise a temporary influence for a year at a time, from one birthday to the next. Harmonizing yourself with these unfolding cycles enables you to make the most of opportunities, taking appropriate action, and to know when it is necessary to wait quietly for a more auspicious cycle to begin. Many people ask about moving when what they really want is to change their lives. They feel that if they move, they will leave all their problems behind them. Needless to say, the problems soon reassert themselves. It is much better to consult an oracle as to what changes need to be made before you move and then look for a house that will bring out the best in you.

Runes

If you are seeking to know whether it is time for a move, take a single rune from your rune pouch (see pages 166–9). Watch out for:

Othila (Reversed) could well signal problems with property deals. It might be better to wait a while.

Ehwaz With its connection to travel could well indicate a long distance move or a job abroad.

Thurisaz It might be better to concentrate on inner moves before making an outer one.

Ansuz Time for a move.

Jera A fresh start. Good time to house hunt.

Eithwaz Period of waiting. Sale or purchase may be slow to occur; something could intervene.

Numerology

If you understand the nine-year cycles of numerology, you can use them to find an auspicious year to move or to start a new project. Your Personal Year Vibration Number shows the phase you are in. While it may be frustrating to wait for a year or so before you move, the flow of your own personal cycle helps you to maximize the potential of each year.

To find your Personal Year Vibration Number:
Write down your day and month of birth.
Write down the current year (in full).
Add each of the digits together until you reach a single number.

Example

If you were born on March 14 and it is now 2001, your personal year number is 2 $(3 + 1 + 4 + 2 + 1 = 11 = 1 + 1 = 2)$ — not a good year to move.

The Unfolding Cycle of Nine

Year 1 New Beginnings Start of cycle. Planning, planting. Standing on your own. Initiating, individuating. Self-reliance, independence. Attract mentor. Good time to retrain or buy a house.

Year 2 Co-operation Period of germination. Working with others. Avoid major decisions. Personal matters adjust to partnership needs. Possibility of deception. Not a good time to move.

Year 3 Activity Growth. Social activity. Urge to travel. Act on ideas, get out what you put in. Vulnerability. Over-indulgence: weight gain. Good time to rent.

Year 4 Stability Firm foundations. Put down roots. Review, reflect. Concentrate on work. Acquisition of money and possessions. Clear what is outgrown. Buy.

Year 5 Opportunity First fruits. Active period in all areas. Options, choices. Freedom from routine. Communication highlighted. Sexual magnetism; new relationships. Guard against energy depletion. Good time to move.

Year 6 Vision Share the harvest. Generosity and abundance. Home and family — responsibilities increase. Marriage possible. Legal decisions restore harmony. If differences not reconciled, separation. Good time to buy.

Year 7 Gratitude Period of retreat. Relax, enjoy benefits of your labor. Health and recuperation. Need for solitude. Review past. Good time to study. Stay put or rent.

Year 8 Abundance Reap the harvest. Karmic balancing: advancement or loss. Pressure, responsibility. Could inherit or win money. Intense sexual and spiritual relationships. Wait a year before moving.

Year 9 Completion End of cycle. Winding down, letting go, quiet reflection. Change of job or relocation. Inevitable change. Work for common good. Do not cling to what has been. Good time to move.

Is this the right place for me?

Where should I move to?

Based on a numerical system, Nine Star Ki is extremely useful when moving. It directs you to a favorable area for you to flourish and helps you to avoid harmful directions. You also can select a direction to bring in new energies — those that favor a career move or a new endeavor, such as writing, for example.

Nine Star Ki

The unfolding cycle behind this system means different years offer different auspicious directions depending on your birth number. Each year some directions will be more favorable for you than others, and you can time a move for maximum auspiciousness. Moving in an unfavorable direction will only cause problems.

You first need to know your birth number. Refer to the chart on page 183. If, for example, you were born in March 1949, your birth number is 6.

Then, determine the direction of your new house or place of work from your present one. Look on the chart on page 184 to see if this is a favorable direction for your number. In the year 2002, for example, good directions for a move for the number 6 would be north-northeast, east-northeast, and south.

Magic Moves

In Nine Star Ki, each of the nine numbers is associated with a specific type of energy — some of which may be favorable for your purpose, others not. If you are planning a move, check whether the description of the qualities and activities the numbers promote support your aims. Then move in the direction in which the number is placed on the Magic Square (see page 107).

1 Independence, seclusion, privacy, secrecy, convalescence, healing.

2 Practicality, team-work, consolidation, friendships, harmonious family life.

3 Ambition, confidence, enthusiasm, starting a new business, expansion.

4 Creativity, imagination, persistence, tenacity, new relationships, career, business.

5 This is a powerful energy with unpredictable results, which can include gradual deterioration of health and career. Avoid moving toward or away from 5 in the Nine Star Ki chart for any year.

6 Control, dignity, authority, promotion, leadership, greater responsibilities.

7 Contentment, pleasure, romance, improved financial position, new job.

8 Motivation, clarity about direction, change, working for oneself.

9 Passion, emotion, recognition, raised public profile, self-expression, social life.

Auspicious Numbers

The number of your house affects your future. Certain numbers are particularly auspicious while some are favorable for certain kinds of activity and others not. To find your house number, add all the digits together until you are down to a single figure (unless you are dealing with a master number 11, 22, and 33).

Multiple numbers should ascend in value rather than decrease — 135, for example, is more favorable than 531. If your house has a name rather than a number, calculate the numerological value for the name (see pages 22–24) and check this against the numbers, left.

1 New beginnings. Individuality. Living alone. Developing your Self.

2 Partnership. Living together. Harmonious marriage of opposites.

3 Expansion. Good social life. Beware overspending.

4 Security and stability. Working together for common goals.

5 Freedom. Overcomes stagnation. Improves communication and sex appeal.

6 Family. Social responsibility. Good for home working.

7 Contemplation. Introspection. Difficult for more than one person.

8 Prosperity and abundance. Brings friends, family, and riches. Wholeness and recognition.

9 Humanitarianism and compassion. Completion: end of cycle. Ties up loose ends.

11 Master number of creativity. Particularly good for metaphysical studies.

22 Master number of unlimited potential. Excellent for developing strengths.

33 All things are open to you.

Nine Star Ki

Arising in Japan, Nine Star Ki is based on your birthdate and its interaction with the current year. Nine refers to the nine numbers and ki is the Japanese word for energy. Each of the nine numbers has a particular energy, and this energy can be found in different directions, according to a nine-year cycle. The prevailing energy at your birth is reflected in your birthchart — the square with your birth number in the center (see opposite page). You can use Nine Star Ki to find out more about yourself — not only your characteristics at birth, but also how you will feel each year. As your birth number enters each direction, you take on some of its characteristics. With the aid of the directions, you can make a move to locate a better job, a more compatible relationship, or a harmonious home. You also can plan vacations or business trips in favorable directions. Each year as the cycle unfolds, the suitability of directions changes. The charts on the opposite page show the flow of energy for 2000–2017. Use them to see what the future holds and to plan your actions accordingly.

The Magic Square

Nine Ki Astrology is based on a magic square (the chart with the 5 in the center), which expresses cosmic order and movement. It is so-named because each line of numbers — diagonal, vertical, horizontal — adds up to 15. The numbers are situated in houses, which are associated with directions and seasons. The magic square (and its related charts), functions both as a map and a timetable. Note the position of north — traditional on Japanese maps.

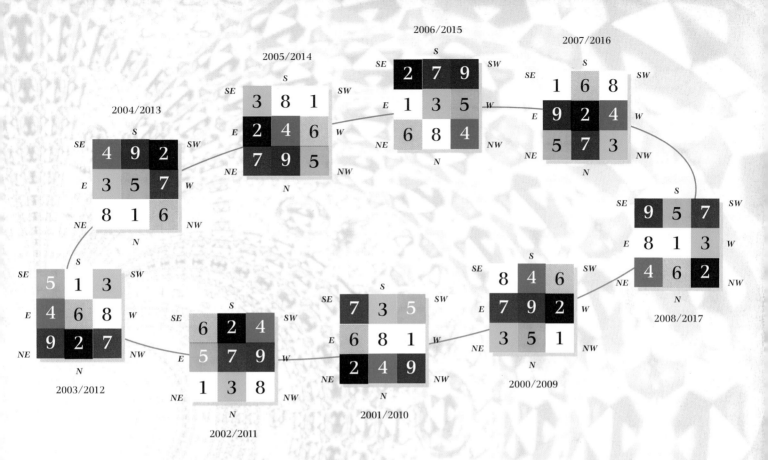

Southeast *Late Spring* Tangible results of previous action. Act when timing appropriate. (Look, think, act.) Good communication.

South *Summer* Fame and fortune. New friends and interests. What you seek to conceal may be revealed. Do not over-extend.

Southwest *Summer to Autumn* A quiet time. Accumulate resources but don't start new ventures yet. Period of worry and over-concern for others.

West *Autumn* Relaxation and easy flow. Remain grounded. Do not be seduced by appearances. Care required in handling money.

Northwest *Autumn to Winter* Forward movement. Past efforts pay off. Do not be over pushy. Avoid accidents and excess heat.

North *Winter* Little movement. Avoid excess activity. Meditate and conserve energy. Finances difficult. Tendency to retreat into oneself.

Northeast *Winter to Spring* Inner depth and stillness. Do not push. Look within. Let go old patterns. Make necessary changes.

East *Spring* New energy awakes. Creativity stimulated. Mentally active — do not overlook details. Act or frustration sets in.

Center *Dangerous house* Either fortunate or unfortunate. May be karmic reckoning of what has gone before. When Natal Year Number falls here, reflect, assess and plan from experience. Do not act yet.

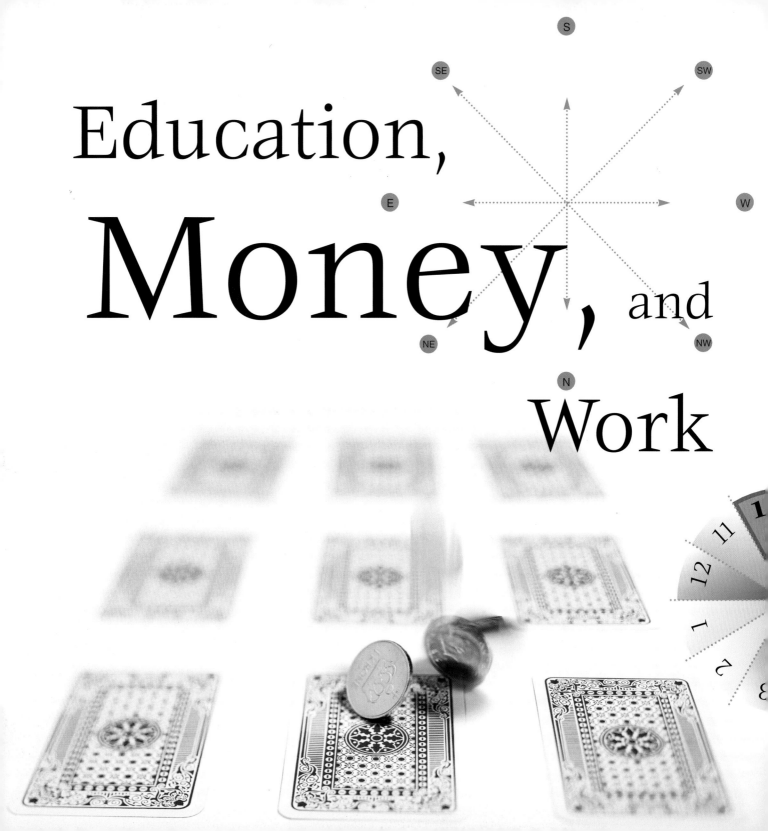

Education, Money, and Work

In times gone by, people had a job for life. It was often a case of following in one's family's footsteps where trades were handed down through the generations. Vocations were mostly limited to the church or the army. Many people received little or no formal education. A lucky few were able to use their innate talents and skills, and even fewer rose beyond their allotted station in life. On-the-job training through craft guilds was available but the majority did what they had to do. Despite this, certain trades became associated with particular signs of the zodiac in the East and West.

Many of the associations came about through the planetary ruler of a sign. The God of War, Mars, for instance, rules the pushy, assertive sign of Aries. Not only is this said to make Aries people good warriors, it also brought in an association with sharp, cutting tools and careers such as butcher or armorer. Metal working, dentistry, and crude surgery also came under the auspices of Mars. Mars also is associated with the secretive birth sign, Scorpio. Not surprisingly, Scorpios are said to make good surgeons and gynecologists. But the discovery of Scorpio's modern ruler, Pluto, has interesting links with sewers and plumbing, and with espionage and surveillance. It refines the crude nature of martian surgery. New career possibilities open up all the time. Today, of course, not only do people often change jobs, but they also have educational options open to them throughout life. Consulting an oracle about these can give you the opportunity to bring a previously unrecognized talent into flower. People also have many more possibilities for careers, including running their own businesses, and divination can give guidance here, too.

Money is a topic of perennial interest, and you can receive advice on how to maximize your money — and how to make your risk taking safer. Indeed, there are oracles that arose specially for this purpose.

What course should I study?

What type of education would be best? What are my abilities?

Ideally, you should train in a field that suits your innate abilities and skills. Knowing what to take as a major or even for extra evening courses is something with which many people are concerned — both for themselves and for their children. Nine Star Ki shows your strengths. The attributes associated with each number become more pronounced as you mature. You don't express them easily, you have to work on them as they are part of your self-actualization: becoming all that you can be. Once you have identified these strengths, however, you can deepen them by appropriate education.

Dowsing down a line of suggested courses can be a quick way to get an answer to which course to take.

Pendulum Dowsing

You can program a pendulum to give you "yes or no" answers to a variety of questions (see page 137). Simply run your finger down a list of options and let your pendulum swing to give you an appropriate answer.

Nine Star Ki

Your Nine Star Ki number defines your underlying character and basic values, and determines your deepest nature. It points to strategies that will enable you to be successful in life and sets out your strengths. An education that promotes and builds up these strengths will help ensure a better career choice (see also page 112) and, ultimately, a happier life. To find your Nine Star Ki number, refer to the chart on page 183. If, for example, you were born in 1985 on or after February 6, you are a number 6. On the other hand, if you were born in the same year but between January 1 and February 5, you are a number 7.

1 **Strengths** Deep thinking, adaptable, able to set limits, motivating, allocating and managing resources, risk-analysis.
Education Spiritual teachings, healing, arts, philosophy, practical skills, herbalism, law, music.

2 **Strengths** Managing, supporting, stabilizing, assimilating, consolidating, anchoring, group work.
Education Psychology, mind-body-spirit, liberal arts, counseling, history, management, music.

3 **Strengths** Ideas, independent thinking, planning, brainstorming, visualizing, organizing, public speaking, environmental scanning.
Education Ecology, science, computer studies, information technology, media studies, creative writing.

The Square of 36

The Square of 36 is a traditional playing card layout that looks at various areas of your life. You can use this layout to do a "life reading" on all aspects, or to answer specific queries.

Method

Frame your question and hold it in your mind.
Shuffle a pack of playing cards and deal into six rows of six as shown.
Each position is concerned with a particular aspect. Check below to see which are relevant to your question, and then look through the following pages to see the suit of the card falling in the position — and its meaning. For example, a heart in position 16, that of marriage, indicates a happy one. If face cards appear in your spread, they can indicate people who are involved (see page 43), so if the heart in position 16 is a Jack, your partner will be a fair-haired young man with blue, gray, or hazel eyes!

4 **Strengths** Ground-breaker, decision making, clarification, scheduling, structuring, time-keeping.
Education Media studies, psychology, marketing, self-development, creative writing.

5 **Strengths** Consolidating, leading, catalyzing, recycling, problem solving, innovating.
Education Counseling, environmental studies, arts, religion, leading-edge subjects.

6 **Strengths** Activating, initiating, inspiring, moral leadership and ethics, balancing, altruistic, leadership.
Education Negotiating skills, philosophy, ethics, jewelry making, counseling, complementary medicine.

7 **Strengths** Evaluating, accounting, managing change, public speaking, detecting subtle trends, esthetics.
Education Public speaking, statistics, conflict resolution, catering, accountancy.

8 **Strengths** Nurturing, supporting, producing, integrating, methodical, single-mindedness, distributing information.
Education Arts, media studies, banking, practical skills, information technology.

9 **Strengths** Prioritizing, networking, problem solving, team building, co-ordinating, relating, leading, communicating, promoting.
Education Media studies, horticulture, fashion design, the arts, information technology.

Should I go seek further schooling?

Do I need to educate myself further? Should I retrain?

With the leaps in technology and possibilities for home working, many people want to know whether they should retrain for another career or whether it is appropriate to go back to school. It's also important to know when to do this and Numerology, with its unfolding progression over nine years, can help you to tune into your own rhythm. Nine Star Ki is an excellent indicator for when would be a good time to go back to school. Astrology, too, provides many pointers.

Western Astrology

Traditionally, the ninth house is connected with higher education. If you are asking whether you should study for a degree, then it is to here you should look. If Jupiter or Mercury is passing through this house on its journey around your chart, it is an excellent time for studying. Mercury speeds up, and Jupiter expands, your mind. However, if you intend to do an evening class or to study at home, one of these planets passing through your third house could also be a good indicator.

If the course is for pleasure and not serious learning, the fifth house could be significant — is this the time you turn a hobby into a career? If your question concerns retraining, then the sixth house, which shows your vocation, is important. Jupiter and Mercury passing through can be helpful here and Saturn can make it imperative to follow your vocation. If you know your birthchart, refer to it for your houses. If not, count your Sun sign as number 1 and count forward counterclockwise the required number of signs. Check the Astrological Tables on pages 185–8 to see when the planets are active.

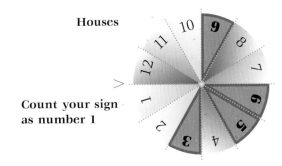

Houses

Count your sign as number 1

3rd house Evening class or home study.
5th house You may want to study for pleasure.
6th house Vocational training or retrain for new career.
9th house Higher education beckons.

Sun signs

♈ *Aries*
♉ *Taurus*
♊ *Gemini*
♋ *Cancer*
♌ *Leo*
♍ *Virgo*
♎ *Libra*
♏ *Scorpio*
♐ *Sagittarius*
♑ *Capricorn*
♒ *Aquarius*
♓ *Pisces*

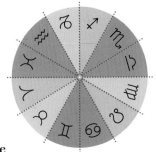

Example
Aries' 3rd house
is Gemini

Numerology

In the course of your Personal Nine-Year Cycle, certain years — 1, 5, and 7 — are good ones in which to study. Other years will be better for different endeavors. See page 97 for a complete explanation of the cycle.

To find out whether you are in a favorable year for study, you need to compute your Personal Year Vibration by writing down your month and day of birth and the current year in full. Add each of the digits together until you reach a single number. So, if you were born May 10 and this is 2002, your personal year number is 1, an auspicious time to go back to school.

1 *st year* An excellent year to begin a course of education or to retrain for another career as the cycle is just beginning. It is a year when you can attract a mentor to guide your footsteps.

5 *th year* An active year, with new possibilities unfolding and communication playing an important part. This too would be a good year for education, especially if it involved leaving home.

7 *th year* Would only be suitable if you were pursuing a solitary course of study where you could work at your own pace within your own home, as it is a time of rest and recuperation.

Nine Star Ki

This ancient Eastern system is an excellent indicator for when would be a good time to go back to school. Each year the prevailing energies change and some are particularly favorable for undertaking further training. You need to find your Nine Star Ki Number. Refer to the chart on page 183. If, for example, you were born in 1972 on or after February 5, you would be a 1. If, however, you were born in the same year between January 1 and February 5, you would be a 2.

The third house, East, on the "Magic Square" (see below) is a creative house. If your Nine Star Ki Number falls here, ideas flood in and the mind is stimulated. If your number is visiting this house (once every nine years), it can be a good time to start wide-ranging, liberal study. As this house is not so conducive to orderly, organized thought with attention to detail, the year is not appropriate to start a major that is tightly focused, scientific, or narrow. Wait until the next year, when your number will fall in the fourth house, Southeast. See pages 100–1 for the changing cycles.

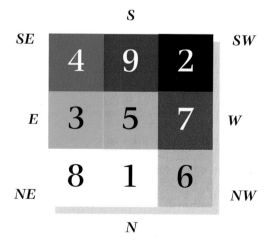

Chinese Astrology

The different animals of Chinese astrology exhibit different qualities, which can be utilized to determine successful career choices. If you don't know your animal, turn to page 182.

Rat

Qualities Energetic, adaptable, versatile, works on several projects. Strong willed, ambitious, pursues goals tenaciously. People-handling skills, friendly persuasion. Good planner and salesperson.

Suitable careers Buying and selling, accountancy, publishing, music, and outdoor pursuits.

Ox

Qualities Logical, organized, stubborn. Does not enjoy competition or wheeler-dealing, preferring meticulous planning and fixed parameters; can rise to challenges.

Suitable careers Horticulture, estate management, medicine, teaching, or law enforcement.

Tiger

Qualities Positive, enthusiastic, optimistic. Enjoys challenges, inspired by chance remarks. Good leader. Plans and tackles jobs head-on, cuts through side issues to core.

Suitable careers Politics, design, travel, law enforcement, advertising, and business.

Rabbit

Qualities Imaginative, intelligent, sensitive. Dislikes competition, pressure, risk, aggression, finance, and "cut and thrust" business. Works well in creative organizations.

Suitable careers The arts, literature, design, public relations, counseling, law.

Dragon

Qualities Charismatic, lively, self-confident. Enjoys responsibility. Exhibits natural authority and leadership. Needs challenges and freedom to expand. Energy can overwhelm colleagues.

Suitable careers Law, the arts, religion, management, medicine.

Snake

Qualities Decisive, independent, logical. Good judge of situations. Organized worker, excellent negotiator. Balances work and play. Spots potential problems and diffuses them.

Suitable careers Politics, public relations, law, psychology, catering, archeology.

Horse

Qualities Confident, independent, friendly. Inspiring leader. Strong constitution suits physically and mentally demanding work. Energies directed to achieving goals. Team-worker as long as contribution is recognized by co-workers.

Suitable careers Sports, construction, politics, actor, sales, or advertising executive.

Ram

Qualities Considerate, creative, sensitive. Ability to turn fortunes around at last minute. Dislikes routine, rigid schedules, competition, too many decisions. Flair for art and creative work. Needs a comfortable niche.

Suitable careers Advertising, research, the arts, librarianship, philosopher.

Monkey

Qualities Versatile, intelligent, quick-witted. Suited to multi-tasking and a wide variety of jobs. Always achieves targets. Good at assessing risk, financial acumen. Enjoys challenges and seeking solutions. Excellent organizational skills.

Suitable careers Finance, media, management, public relations, law enforcement, manual worker, design, planning.

Rooster

Qualities Charming, independent, logical. Confident facade hides vulnerability. Dislikes pressure. Needs freedom to be creative. Well suited to self-employment.

Suitable careers Sales, politics, public relations, writing, entertaining, armed forces.

Dog

Qualities Honest, courageous, responsible. Dislikes aggression, competition, and deadlines. Reliable and conscientious, excellent teamworker. Defender of good causes.

Suitable careers Research, education, law, social or charity work, medicine, campaign worker, counseling.

Pig

Qualities Honest, loyal, supportive. Unambitious, prefers working steadily, avoids taking risks. Dislikes back-stabbing and competition. Needs human contact.

Suitable careers Social work, medicine, law, music, science, landscape gardening, art, librarianship.

In what career will I find success?

What's the right job for me?
To what work am I suited?

Geomancy is an easy way to access information on careers. Astrology, Eastern and Western, is useful when you are deciding which career to pursue or pondering a complete career change. If you combine all three and the same career comes up, then that is the one to go for.

Geomancy

With a pencil or marker, make four lines of random dashes across a piece of paper, one below the other. Put a large dot • at the end of each odd-numbered line and two dots •• at the end of each even-numbered line and check to see if the resulting figure is one of those below.

Puella would suggest working with children.

Populus favors a career with people.

Via working alone.

Laetitia the entertainment industry.

Rubeus the armed forces.

For other geomantic figures, see pages 80–3.

Sun Signs

Aries Fireman, arms dealer, foundry worker, metal worker, prospector, car mechanic, explorer, psychiatrist, engineer, astronaut, butcher, dentist, surgeon, entrepreneur, wheeler-dealer, union official, sportsperson, motor racer, test pilot, long distance truck driver, electrician, electronic engineer, eco-warrior.

Taurus Restaurant critic, restaurateur, masseur, singer, musician, landscape gardener, horticulturist, organic farmer, surveyor, builder, art or antique dealer, body artist, jeweler, sculptor, architect, craftworker, businessperson, government employee, administrator, financier, banker, investment broker, pensions administrator, real estate broker, office manager.

Gemini Journalist, broadcaster, lecturer, teacher, linguist, navigator, civil engineer, commentator, mailperson, sales representative or assistant, personal assistant, travel agent, craftsperson, messenger, wheeler-dealer, bookseller, advertising agent, demonstrator, spin doctor, internet salesman, mobile phone salesperson, communications expert.

Cancer Social worker, nursery nurse, nanny, midwife, homeworker, careworker, human resources personnel, housing officer, nurse, kindergarten teacher, hotelier, caterer, chef, boatbuilder, antique dealer, fisherman, sailor, museum curator, businessperson, historian, real estate agent, interior designer, textile designer.

Leo Actor, dancer, film or television producer, television presenter, fashion model, rock star, fashion designer, window dresser, solar heating engineer, goldsmith, gold dealer, jeweler, sportsperson, youth worker, teacher, politician, president, managing director, lawyer, fundraiser, judge, play-therapist, bond dealer, cardiologist, cardiac surgeon.

 Virgo Health professional, hygienist, hygiene operative, personal assistant, analyst, scientist, inspector, writer, craftsperson, gardener, critic, shop assistant, accountant, teacher, linguist, pharmacist, research worker, librarian, computer operator, bookkeeper, dietician, nutritionist, data processor, market researcher, proof reader, management trainer, Feng shui consultant, yoga teacher, statistician.

 Libra Interior decorator, set designer, graphic artist, image consultant, beautician, model, property valuer, dress designer, diplomat, hairdresser, welfare worker, lawyer, judge, receptionist, art dealer, music business, personal shopping consultant, conciliator, dating agency employee, management consultant, negotiator, veterinarian, sex therapist, agent, air steward(ess).

 Scorpio Forensic scientist, surveillance, private investigator, midwife, doctor, pathologist, gynecologist, psychiatrist, psychologist, undertaker, hospice worker, insurance broker, pharmacist, businessperson, butcher, army personnel, research worker, hypnotherapist, sewage worker, law enforcement agent, complementary medicine practitioner, sex therapist, nuclear weapons designer, submariner, diver.

 Sagittarius Philosopher, philosophy therapist, jockey, horse trainer, casino operative, lecturer, teacher, interpreter, publisher, writer, professor, travel guide or agent, librarian, priest, guru, lawyer, sportsperson, bookseller, public relations personnel, personal trainer, sports worker, Feng shui consultant, cosmologist, airline pilot.

 Capricorn CEO, government employee, politician, administrator, law enforcement agent, teacher, builder, bank manager, planner, mathematician, engineer, geologist, farmer, surveyor, architect, orthopedic surgeon, osteopath, chiropracter, dentist, scientist, musician, archeologist, historian, biographer, pensions administrator, geriatric careworker, insurance agent, comedian.

 Aquarius Scientist, quantum physicist, electronic engineer, technologist, ecological consultant, vulcanologist, radiographer, writer, astrologer, astronomer, astronaut, inventor, sociologist, archeologist, anthropologist, researcher, social or charity worker, reformer, cognitive therapist, systems analyst, magician, futures trader.

 Pisces Actor, dancer, artist, illusionist, poet, writer, photographer, animator, fantasy writer, hypnotherapist, intuitive healer, tarot reader, shoe designer, maker or seller, chiropodist, podiatrist, priest, nurse, alcohol or drug counselor, sailor, ship's doctor, cruise organizer, fishmonger.

Nine Star Ki

This form of Eastern astrology also can give you career advice. Each of the nine numbers exhibits particular strengths (see page 104). A career choice that makes the best use of these abilities will enable you to shine. This can have the knock-on effect of making you feel happier and more satisfied in your job — and with life in general. To determine your Nine Star Ki Number, refer to the chart on page 183. If, for example, you were born in 1977 on or after February 4, you are a 5. If, however, you were born in the same year between January 1 and February 4, you are a 6.

1 Healer, social worker, printer, chemist, massage therapist, philosopher, writer, oilman, restaurant owner, waiter, lawyer, maintenance worker, consultant, musician, artist.

2 Shaman, doctor, antique dealer, gardener, supermarket worker, civil engineer, farmer, union representative, public service worker, personnel counseling, estate agent, musician, recruitment.

3 Inventor, technical designer, electronic engineer, construction worker, television personnel, engineer, musician, sportsperson, surgeon, teacher, writer, environmental consultant, scientist, architect, software designer.

4 Advertising and public relations personnel, designer, film director, editor, writer, travel agent, businessperson, communicator, teacher, manufacturer, removals, constructor, media executive, marketing consultant.

5 Politician, mediator, entrepreneur, construction worker, power broker, military personnel, law enforcement agent, refuse collector, secondhand dealer.

6 CEO, military commander, government service, management consultant, machinery operator, lawyer, jeweler, salesperson, teacher, counselor, campaigner, compensation claim administrator, politician, healer, organizer.

7 Public relations, entertainment business, night club owner, banker, lecturer, bartender, dentist, catering or food production, diplomat, quality control, personnel, counseling, stockbroking, jeweler.

8 Writer, artist, artisan, optometrist, book dealer, public servant, politician, law, advertising and public relations, horticulturist, beautician, sales co-ordinator, fashion designer, actor, comedian.

9 Financial trader, sculptor, service worker, government worker, law enforcement agent, banker, teacher, beauty therapist, cleric, property developer, insurance salesperson, actor.

Will I get a job soon?

Geomancy

You can use the quick geomantic method to find an answer. With a soft pencil or marker, make four lines of random dashes across a piece of paper, one below the other. Put a large dot at the end of each odd numbered line and two dots at the end of each even numbered one. If your figure looks like either of the ones below, your chances are good.

  Albus A new job possibility.

Fortuna Major You will get that important job.

Dominoes

Dominoes are another quick and easy way to answer career questions such as "Will I get a job soon?" Use the full set, think of your question, and pull one at random.

 Six-Five Unemployed: a new job soon. Employed: promotion.

 Double Six Extremely favorable for career matters.

 Six-Two New job must be above board to succeed.

 Double Four Favorable for manual work only.

 Four-One Look around for hidden opportunities.

See overleaf for further information.

The Saturn Return

The planet Saturn is Lord of Karma. A great teacher, it takes roughly twenty-eight years to move around the birth chart and return to its natal place. Most people have at least two Saturn Returns during their lifetimes. The Saturn Return is a major period of reassessment in your life. You look at what you have done up to now and see whether it is really in accord with your life path and your ambitions. If it is not, you may have to make some drastic changes.

At the First Saturn Return, age 28–29, you may go back to school or retrain for a different career. You might suddenly become ambitious, or decide to settle down. You may move out of your relationship or find a new set of friends.

At the Second Saturn Return, age 57–58, you may find yourself redundant or facing retirement and yet having many years of active life in front of you. You could take up voluntary work or go back to school.

Whatever happens at the Return, Saturn is a stern taskmaster and if you do not fulfill your life plan at this time, you could well slip into apathy and Saturnine gloom. Indeed, many people find themselves entering into a period of depression. If it happens to you, take time to look within to see what changes are demanded.

Dominoes

Found in the tombs of Egypt, dominoes are one of our oldest games. It is likely that they were used for divination from their earliest days. There are certain superstitions attaching to divination by dominoes. It is said they should be used no more than once a month and never on a Monday or Friday. A single domino is useful when you need fast guidance but, when seen as a spread of three, they can be surprisingly informative.

Method
Place the full set of dominoes face down on a table. Swirl them around. Concentrate on your question. Pick one for a fast answer, three for more detailed information.

Double Six Favorable for career or business. Love and finance prosper. Happy relationships, child. Caring, helpful parents. Fortunate for property.

Six-Five Going up in world. Opposition from friends; may be trouble involving children. If out of work, job soon. Relationships good but need work.

Six-Four Prosperity ahead but beware those who would rob you. Early, happy, and secure marriage, children follow soon. Legal matters in near future.

Six-Three Strong intent wins. Stable relationships, marriage to reliable partner. Successful journey. Good news of vehicle. Possible illness in middle age.

Six-Two Good things waiting, do not let fear intervene. Hardworking, sensible partner. Excellent for love affairs and marriage. Useful gift will arrive. Irregular business deals fail.

Six-One Things never are as bad as they could be. Two marriages, second happier. Children prosper and travel. Problem solved. Happiness in mid-age.

Six-Blank Love affairs bring happiness. Jealousy and gossip abound. Accidents possible. News of a death.

Double Five Changes to come. Fortunate house move. Health improves. Excellent career. Luck, money, happy marriage.

Five-Four Money problems, possibly associated with partner. Work provides independence and prosperity.

Five-Three Money gained by hard work although you will never be short of money. Relationships reasonably happy. Pleasant visitor.

Five-Two Married life source of comfort if you act well; if made for money it is cool. Possibility of unrequited love. News of childbirth. New enterprises.

Five-One Happiness awaits: parties, social events. Family ties or riches but not both. Money problems may be long-term. Charismatic, short-lived relationship.

Five-Blank Avoid speculation and love affairs, you get your fingers burnt. Friend may need shoulder to cry on.

Double Four Determination takes you a long way. Favorable for manual work, not professional. Young people, parties, sports, social events on the horizon.

Four-Three Financial situation undergoes change. Disappointments concerning children. Illness possible. Difficulties with vehicle.

Four-Two Traveling brings success and pleasure. Unexpected events concerning home and family — good or bad. Beware of flirt or philanderer.

Four-One Watch for road to success which you could easily miss. Good marriage, but possibly no children. Bills to pay.

Four-Blank Watch out in matters of love. Relationship problems, temporary reconciliation. Twins in family. New outlook on life.

Double Three Life offers great deal. Money soon: legacy, win, or bonus. Do not throw away chances. Outside interference leads to short-term relationship problems.

Three-Two Excellent for new enterprise. Rise above petty worries. Love life prospers. Enjoyable journey. Don't take chances, dishonesty revealed.

Three-One Good news. A surprise. Business matters cause apprehension but turn out well. Possibility of love affair gets you into trouble.

Three-Blank Domestic problems due to weak partner or family member. Jealousy, broken friendships. Keep your heart open.

Double Two Partnerships go well. You derive joy from marriage and family. Watch your health.

Two-One Marry in haste, repent at leisure. Business loss or failure, possibly home too. Passionate but disastrous love affair.

Two-Blank Entangling of marriage and money. Beware thieves. Proceed cautiously, relationships not good. Successful outcome to journey. Sales, communications do well.

Double One You will be happy where you are. Decision takes courage. Happy family life, helpful parents. Luck, money, love.

One-Blank Luck comes in unexpected manner. Danger of money or resources being wasted. Visitor from overseas. Improvement in health.

Double Blank Trouble on way could affect job, health, relationships. Beware of accidents. Disappointment, loss, theft.

Am I in the right job?

Do I need to make changes in my working life?

Am I going to encounter difficulties?

You may well find yourself looking to change your career. Palmistry can be a quick indicator and Astrology can provide reassurance. The I Ching and The Square of 36 can answer a variety of questions concerning work.

Palmistry
Certain lines on your hand can indicate whether you are the type of person who stays in a job for life or when you simply must change your job.

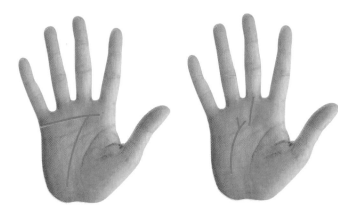

Job-for-life   **Must-change-job**

I Ching
The hexagrams in the classic Chinese oracle can indicate problems in your work life. To create a hexagram, you will need to throw three coins six times. Each time there is a majority of heads, draw an unbroken line and each time there is a majority of tails, draw a broken line. Build up from the bottom. See if your resulting hexagram looks like the following:

 18 Work on What Is Spoiled A false impression must be corrected.

 20 Watchfulness Concentrate on the overall picture not the details.

 22 Grace Time to spruce up your image.

 33 Retreat Admit your choice was wrong and retreat.

 35 Progress Promotion.

 40 Disentangling Situation comes to a head, you know where you stand.

 44 Meeting Something is weakening your situation.

 48 The Well You may have miscalculated a situation.

 52 Stillness Stay out of sight and avoid being noticed.

 60 Restriction Stay small. Not a time for big ambitions.

 63 Final Completion Do not lose through stupidity what you have gained.

Western Astrology

Astrology can help reassure you that your career is congenial and will be successful. The sixth house is the work that you must do, your vocation, and the tenth house is your career. If you know the placement of Jupiter in your birthchart, then you have a pointer to where success can be found. If it is in your sixth or tenth house, expect a spectacular career. Jupiter passing through the tenth house by transit often acts to kick-start your career and indicates a prime opportunity. If you do not know your birthchart, you can place your Sun sign at the start of the first house (see chart below) and count counterclockwise to the sixth or the tenth house. Then refer to the Astrological Tables on pages 185–8 to check the movement of Jupiter.

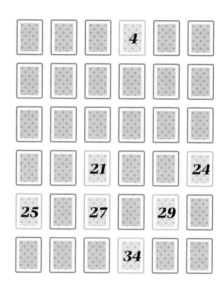

Houses

Count your sign as number 1

Sun signs

♈ *Aries*

♉ *Taurus*

♊ *Gemini*

♋ *Cancer*

♌ *Leo*

♍ *Virgo*

♎ *Libra*

♏ *Scorpio*

♐ *Sagittarius*

♑ *Capricorn*

♒ *Aquarius*

♓ *Pisces*

Example
Aries' 6th house is Virgo

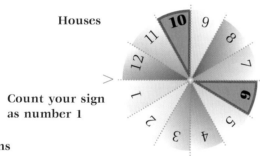

The Square of 36

This is a very specific playing card layout that can be extremely useful for asking a number of questions concerning work. Shuffle a full pack of cards and deal six rows of six cards.

If you ask any of the following questions, refer to the indicated positions — as these will have relevance — then check the significance of the suit that appears in that place by referring to pages 118–22.

4, 24 "Will I get this promotion?"

34 "Will I get a raise?"

27 "Is this a good time to give notice?"

21 "Will I regret this decision?"

25, 29 "Will my boss stand up for me?"

The Positions

1 **Prospects (immediate)** Project currently engaged in.

2 **Accomplishments** What you gain.

3 **Recognition** Gauge of success.

4 **Expectations** Hopes in the balance.

5 **Speculations** Risks you are taking.

6 **Wishful thinking** What you cannot gain by own efforts.

7 **Injustices** Grievances/injustices and how to rectify them.

8 **Ingratitude** Worries.

9 **Contacts** Fellow workers, business partners, etc.

10 **Reverses** Warnings cards offer.

11 **Problems** Petty personal annoyances to business affairs.

12 **Assets** Personal effects, job security, property, bonds.

13 **Joy** Where it will come from.

14 **Love** Relationship to close companions.

15 **Prosperity** Immediate and future.

16 **Marriage** Future or present (dependent on age).

17 **Worries** From trivial to deep-rooted concerns.

18 **Harmony** How to find it.

19 **Windfalls** Unexpected good fortune.

20 **Deception** Higher the card, bigger the deception. Picture cards point to perpetrators

21 **Opposition** Competition or conflict.

22 **Gifts** Tokens of esteem.

23 **Friendship** Dependability of those you trust.

24 **Advancement** Improving status or attainments.

25 **Co-operation** How much you can depend on outside aid under pressure.

26 **Success** Long-range undertakings.

27 **Change** Advantages and disadvantages.

28 **Sadness** Endings, doom and disasters.

29 **Rewards** Appreciation for services rendered.

30 **Scandal** Events affecting your reputation.

31 **Prospects (long term)** Potential and lucky breaks.

32 **Affluence** Money, wealth, and solvency.

33 **Neglect** Ignored opportunities.

34 **Awards** Favors, raises, etc.

35 **Influence** How far ambition takes you.

36 **Health** Accidents or illness.

hearts

1   Proceed to success.
2   Satisfaction exceeds expectations.
3   Success and recognition.
4   Expectations fulfilled more than anticipated.
5   Unexpected gains, follow hunches.
6   Deepest desire realized much sooner than expected.
7   Wrongs soon remedied and turned to advantage.
8   Appreciation will soon be expressed.
9   Everything is for the best, profit is assured.
10 Loss of something you have depended on too strongly.
11 Disputes with friends/family could be serious. Handle with tact.
12 Sudden upturn and increase.
13 Inspiration and appreciation of finer things in life.
14 Utter contentment and mutual understanding.

hearts

15 Aim for big goal. Prosperity is yours to extent you deserve it.
16 Happy marriage, mutual interests, greater understanding. **Ace** romance.
17 Worries close to home soon pass.
18 Do not neglect close friendships which bring mutual benefits.
19 Outstanding gift or opportunity, longer it takes, better it is.
20 Scheme against you backfires on perpetrators.
21 Complete triumph over all and any obstacles.
22 High honors or fine gifts beyond expectations.
23 Close friends or lovers utterly trustworthy.
24 Sudden promotion, rapid rise, fame, and honor. If success limited by surroundings, make a change.
25 You only have to ask. Aid from unexpected sources.

hearts

26 Success in well-planned projects, more ambitious the better.
27 Opportune change for better. Follow hunches.
28 Learn something totally unexpected as result of a death.
29 Reward far beyond expectations.
30 Criticism from others for mistakes soon blows over.
31 Lucky streak, take advantage.
32 Business or speculation brings big bank roll.
33 Indifference to others lets own interests lag. Snap out of it.
34 Wealthier your connections, bigger awards to come.
35 All the influence and power you seek.
36 Indisposition brief and trifling.

clubs

1   Prospects good but help of friends needed.
2   Strengthening of friendships outweighs dubious factors.
3   Recognition you deserve comes through friends.
4   Hopes depend on friends old and new, be persistent.
5   Luck if you follow sound advice from reliable people.
6   If you don't get what you want, want what you can get.
7   Friends act as go-betweens to sort out misunderstandings.
8   Approach ingrates through mutual friends to receive appreciation.
9   To avoid loss, keep transactions on friendly basis.
10 You may lose a good friend, a setback to your plans.
11 Serious misunderstandings could force a break.
12 Prosper through own effort and aid from good friends.

Q K A 2 3 4 5 6 7 8 9 10 J Q K A 2 3 4 5 6 7 8 9 10

2 3 4 5 6 7 8 9 10 11 12 13 14 15 16 17 18 19 20 21 22 23 24 25 26 27 28 29 30 31 32 33 34 35

clubs

13 Everyday affairs enhanced by friendship and pride in work.

14 Those you love are dependable and true.

15 Continue to work hard, accept help and advice to gain prosperity.

16 Marriage arranged through friends.

17 Conflict with close friend must be smoothed over.

18 Nurture friendships to advantage.

19 Friend remembers you. One gift foreshadows another.

20 Seek advice if you suspect double-dealing. Tables turned.

21 Keen rivalry. When friends aid, overcome opponents.

22 Generous friends or relatives bring practical gifts.

23 You can totally depend on a close friend.

24 Advancement depends on how hard you work and on friends.

25 Sincere friends aid you, don't overtax them.

clubs

26 Accept offer of friend, seek reliable advice on offer from outsider.

27 With backing of friends, success in financial undertaking. To do it alone is unwise.

28 Death of a friendship or acquaintance.

29 Loyal friends show much-deserved appreciation.

30 **10, J, Q, K, Ace** disgrace of friend causes problems. Lower cards: own dishonor.

31 Opportunity arises through friends.

32 Hard work, brains, and good deals raise income bracket.

33 You neglect friends but feel they are neglectful. Renew old acquaintances.

34 Sincerely further friendships and friends reward you.

35 Authority comes through friends.

36 Impending illness.

diamonds

1 Obstacles, especially in business or finance.

2 Satisfaction may be diminished by petty spite.

3 Partial success may pave way forward.

4 More trifling your hope, the less success.

5 Losses offset by unexpected gains. Pursue money due or lose it.

6 Wildest wishes only partly realized despite help from friends.

7 Be cordial to those who wronged you, they make amends.

8 Look for real reason behind ingratitude, take appropriate steps.

9 Do not take sides or you could be blamed. Use tact.

10 Imminent threat of loss of money or property.

11 Arguments involving money or obligations.

12 Expect opposition or problems over property. Time wasted is golden opportunity lost.

13 Overcome worry and personal conflicts to find joy.

diamonds

14 Clash of interests may produce resentment and mistrust. A rival for affection.

15 Welfare affected by envious schemers. Keep alert.

16 Jealousy and conflict must be overcome for happy marriage.

17 Anger, uncertainty, and strife cause disharmony.

18 Avoid jealousy and arguments with friends or lose them.

19 Rights disputed. Stronger your case, more it costs. Be happy with what you have.

20 Remain calm, fraud or conspiracy collapses with little loss.

21 Disputes among rivals work to your advantage and overcome odds. Triumph over adversity.

22 Unwanted gifts make you indebted, return.

23 Disagreements among friends are not to your advantage. Use humor.

24 Determination needed to counteract criticism and overcome competition. Act swiftly or chances ruined.

J Q K A 2 3 4 5 6 7 8 9 10 J Q K A 2 3 4 5 6 7 8 9

2 3 4 5 6 7 8 9 10 11 12 13 14 15 16 17 18 19 20 21 22 23 24 25 26 27 28 29 30 31 32 33 34

The Square of 36 (continued)

diamonds

25 Co-operation is not forthcoming unless you are honorable.

26 Avoid change, will not work out, may cause contention.

27 Avoid competition, seek success in new area. Ensure all parties in accord, disputes bring failure.

28 Sudden death causes change in plans.

29 Sudden honor which may be belittled by some.

30 Spite, malice and jealousy create commotion. Keep low profile.

31 Jealousy aimed against you turns to your favor.

32 Money made but may not come your way. Be warned.

33 Careless attitude weakens own position, strengthens others.

34 People lend money, or offer opportunity instead of bonus. Take it.

35 Aims blocked by envy. Secretly further ambition but don't expect full success.

36 Bout of well known ailment.

spades

1 Delays, failure due to misplaced confidence.

2 Unfair tactics, or fraud, lessen satisfaction.

3 Antagonism and underhand methods leave little satisfaction.

4 No possibility of fulfillment. Abandon or things get worse.

5 Avoid risks no matter how sound — bankruptcy or robbery likely. Keep up insurance.

6 No chance.

7 Injustice worsens if you try to right it. Ignore.

8 You have been too generous to the ungrateful. Avoid similar mistakes in future.

9 Trust only yourself. Take immediate profit not future promises. Others may be squeezing you out.

10 Important interests at stake: watch out for wheeler-dealers. Lack of foresight brings misery and remorse.

11 Envy and enmity create anguish.

12 Sacrifice much unless you work twice as hard.

spades

13 Help others and help yourself. Loyalty rewarded through people in high places. **Ace** disappointment.

14 Love is fickle. Perseverance could overcome, but is it worth it?

15 Progress hampered by interference and antagonism. Counteract.

16 Marriage may be broken up by others. **7**, **8**, or **9** divorce.

17 Vicious critics or deadly enemies. Action futile, allow situation to disperse.

18 Superficial friendships, move on, keep options open to renew.

19 You may have been defrauded of forgotten or unknown property. Discover truth now.

20 Reputation could be ruined by double dealing and deception.

21 You are being outwitted and outclassed.

22 "Free gifts" have a catch. Avoid shady schemes.

23 Beware misplaced affection, false friends. Rely on proven friends.

spades

24 Rivals block with malicious tactics, obstacles too great for fame. Undertake lesser duties capably and something bigger may arise.

25 Competitors usurp proffered aid. Get by on your own or go elsewhere.

26 Unforeseen difficulties. Let others take risks..

27 Hold onto present position as unscrupulous people trying to push you out.

28 Sudden death solves pressing problem.

29 You will not receive rewards you anticipate.

30 Rough time whether in right or wrong.

31 Danger, beware. Friends aid but nerves shattered.

32 Profits intercepted. Take what you make and work to keep it.

33 Take care of possessions or lose everything.

34 You will receive nothing.

35 Ambition is wishful thinking, unattainable.

36 Ill health may affect social and business life.

Where should I look for work?

If you are having difficulty finding employment, then use your Chinese animal direction to guide your search. If you don't know your year animal, turn to page 182.

Chinese Astrology

Rat North

Ox North-northeast

Tiger East-northeast

Rabbit East

Dragon East-southeast

Snake South-southeast

Horse South

Ram South-southwest

Monkey West-southwest

Rooster West

Dog West-northwest

Pig North-northwest

Prophetic Coin

The Prophetic Coin is an oracle from antiquity. In those days it was thrown onto squares drawn on the earth, but today it is easier to use playing cards on a table top. This versatile oracle can throw light on underlying difficulties as well as pointing the way forward and giving good advice for the future.

You will need a bright, shiny coin with distinctly different sides so that you can read "heads" and "tails," together with nine cards.

Method
- Shuffle the cards and lay out face down in three rows of three; leave space about the width of your coin between the cards and rows.

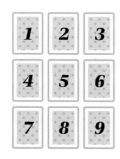

- Hold the coin edgewise, a foot or so above the center of the cards.
- Drop the coin and allow it to roll into place.
- Note whether the coin has landed heads or tails up.
- If it has landed on a card, read its meaning. If the coin does not land on a card, wait a few days before trying again.

Card 1
Heads Time for you to take decisive and independent action to achieve what you want.
Tails Do not under any circumstances be talked into doing something you do not want to do. Someone is trying to use you for their advantage.

Card 2
Heads An opportunity awaits your decision, which will turn out well. Time to give advice rather than take it.
Tails Not a good time to help anyone in a worse position than yourself. You will be blamed for stirring up trouble.

Card 3
Heads Reassess what you are planning. It can be done in a better way. To continue as it is is to risk failure.
Tails Keep your ideas quiet for the time being or you may find them appropriated or laughed at by others.

Card 4
Heads Complete one task before starting another. There is a danger of giving up a sure thing for something risky.
Tails You have the practical ability to turn other people's wild ideas into a profitable scheme.

Card 5
Heads Do not be distracted from your set course of action by itchy feet or a desire to have fun. You may regret it.
Tails Avoid gambling and speculation or advantage will be taken of you.

Card 6

Heads Excellent time to settle down to a quiet life, particularly if it makes someone else happy, too.

Tails Do not let other people increase demands on you. You have been too easy-going. Stand firm.

Card 7

Heads Follow your intuition, back your hunches, but do not force things. If you do not know what to do, sit tight and wait it out.

Tails Do not allow gloom or despondency to drive away those who can help you. Keeping cheerful attracts those who can aid your plans.

Card 8

Heads Your plans are not big enough. Keep them practical, but expand, especially where money is concerned.

Tails Business opportunity is coming your way soon. Stash away all the cash you can now so that you can take advantage when it arrives.

Card 9

Heads Your powers of persuasion are at their greatest now. They can gain you what you want, but be sure intentions are honorable or you will have to answer for it later.

Tails Do not let anything disturb your equilibrium. Face up to things, state your case clearly, and you will win.

How can I maximize my money?

I earn a lot but it never seems to be enough, why?

Will I inherit money?

Money has always been a major concern. People want to know how to get it, how to hold on to it, what to do with it, and, just occasionally, how to give it away. There are oracles for all these questions. Astrology can give you valuable pointers — if you know your birthchart and are fortunate enough to have Jupiter in your second house, you always will be able to manifest the money you need. The planets passing through favorable houses also can indicate luck with money and your Sun sign can illuminate your attitude toward it.

Western Astrology

In astrology, the second house is the house of personal resources and the eighth house that of legacies and joint money. Planets passing through these houses stimulate your money issues. If Jupiter is on the move, it might be a case of easy come, easy go. When Saturn passes through the second house, you tend to want to hold onto what money you have, as Saturn can point to severe restrictions in personal finances. When this planet passes through the eighth house, however, there is every chance you may inherit under the terms of a will.

If you do not know your birthchart, counting your Sun sign as number 1, count counterclockwise one or seven signs to find your second or eighth house. Consult the Astrological Tables (pages 185–8) to see when Jupiter and Saturn are passing through these houses.

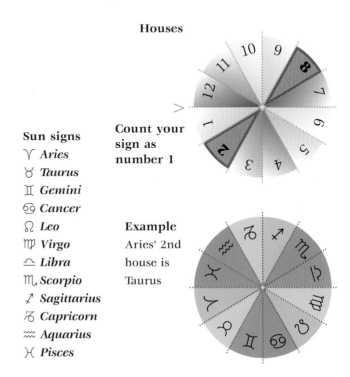

Houses

Count your sign as number 1

Sun signs

♈ *Aries*

♉ *Taurus*

♊ *Gemini*

♋ *Cancer*

♌ *Leo*

♍ *Virgo*

♎ *Libra*

♏ *Scorpio*

♐ *Sagittarius*

♑ *Capricorn*

♒ *Aquarius*

♓ *Pisces*

Example
Aries' 2nd house is Taurus

Sun Signs

 Aries   Impulse buys, little thought for future.

 Taurus   Amasses money in bank.

 Gemini   Easy come, easy go, easy come.

 Cancer   Feels broke unless a few thousand in bank.

 Leo   Lavish spender.

 Virgo   Budgets and plans.

 Libra   Careful, spends on quality.

 Scorpio   "What's mine is mine."

 Sagittarius   Spendthrift, gambler.

 Capricorn   Always something put away for a rainy day.

 Aquarius   Tightfisted.

 Pisces   Flows in, and out again.

Prediction and Divination

Although the terms are often used interchangeably, prediction and divination are different. Prediction assesses the possibility of something happening. It is based on thousands of years of observation and correlation of patterns with events. Economists or investors use statistics and financial indicators to predict, and take advantage of, trends. They need to foresee future events such as a stock market crash to minimize damage. Financial astrology is an exact science based on equally close observation. An astrologer would use different tables than an economist, but could be equally, if not more, accurate in predicting both up and down turns. Divination literally means to seek divine guidance. This is done through what often appears to be random chance or the working of fate. When you consult the Wheel of Destiny (see page 132) about speculation, for instance, you are divining what the future could hold. The ancients believed that God (or the gods) influenced the outcome. Nowadays we are more likely to believe that our subconscious mind is influencing the oracle.

Should I chance my luck?

Should I buy a lottery ticket?

Should I visit the casino?

Should I speculate?

Should I buy stocks and shares?

Should I invest in a risky project?

Everyone dreams of playing to win and many people ask if they should buy a lottery or raffle ticket, while others wonder if they should chance their luck at roulette. A more appropriate way to frame this question might be "If I chance my luck, will I win?" as otherwise you could find yourself receiving an affirmative answer, but still not winning!

Other areas of speculation include buying stocks and shares, investing in risky new projects, taking a chance that an item will turn out to be valuable, or knowing who to trust with your money. You might even want to know if that sales bargain is such a bargain after all. Oracles can indicate a fortunate period in your life. If you are looking for a quick answer, Dominoes can point the way. The Wheel of Destiny, however, offers very precise advice. If the signs point to yes, you could ascertain lucky numbers using Floating Numbers.

Dominoes

You only need to pick one domino to find a quick answer. Place your dominoes face down on the table and shuffle them around. Select one at random and turn it face up. One of the following will be extremely lucky. If yours isn't one of these, see pages 114–15 for the answer.

 Double Six Extremely auspicious; it presages success.

 Double Four Money coming your way.

 Six-Four Prosperity ahead.

Fortunate Days

This system combines astrology and numerology to ascertain those days of the week that will be luckier for you than others. If your birthdate and the current date are in harmony, good fortune can be the result.

To find your Birthdate Number, add together the individual digits of the day, month, and year of your date of birth to get a single-digit number.

Then add together the individual digits of the date in question, again ending with a single digit.

Now look at the charts on pages 139–56. First find your Birthdate Number, then the Day Number, and finally the day of the week in question.

If, for example, your Birthdate Number is 1, and the Day Number is 5 and it falls on a Tuesday, this is a good day to take chances!

The Wheel of Destiny

Using a pin is a time-honored way of making choices. The Wheel of Destiny (see overleaf) focuses your questions into specific areas of life. If, for example, you want to know whether you should invest in a lottery ticket, take your seat at the poker table, or put a fiver on the chestnut filly, the area of Speculation is the one to use, though not all answers pertain. If the answer isn't quite to your liking, you may like to try Fortune as well.

To use the wheel to find out the answer, place the forefinger of one hand underneath the point of Speculation (or Fortune).
Close your eyes and stick a pin in the area above your finger.
Now check the list overleaf to see what your number reveals about whether or not you should try your luck.

Which numbers should I choose?

Floating numbers

Knowing which numbers to choose on your lottery or raffle ticket or at a roulette table is just as important, if not more, than knowing whether to try your luck at all. Follow the easy method below to pick your lucky combinations.

Tear some clean paper into as many squares as there are possible numbers. If you were doing the English lottery, for example, you would need 49 pieces of paper, for a roulette table only 38 — 1 to 36 plus 0 and 00.

Using an indelible pen, write a number on each square. Place the numbers in a bowl and pour over a jug of water.
Retrieve the numbers that rise to the top first. These have the greatest chance of winning.
You can adapt Floating Numbers to give you names of horses or anything else you want to take a gamble on.

The Wheel of Destiny

This oracle can be used both to answer specific questions and also to give you a general idea about what lies in store for you.

The Wheel is divided into eight areas and beneath each one, the numbers one to six are laid out in a particular sequence. To find out the answer to a specific question, first ascertain the area of the Wheel that is most appropriate. For example, if you want to know whether now is the time to enter into a particular business arrangement, you need to use the area of Commerce. In some circumstances, say if you wanted to find out whether you should change your job or not, more than one area may be useful, in this case, Fortune and Commerce.

Method

Once you have your question framed, place the forefinger of one hand beneath the appropriate zone. Then close your eyes and stick a pin into the area above your finger. It should touch or penetrate one of the numbers. To find out what this number means, check below.

Speculation
1 Success in the lottery.
2 Never speculate.
3 Chance luck.
4 Fortunate at cards.
5 Lucky ventures in commerce.
6 Luck in a wager.

Fortune
1 Changes every 7 years.
2 A steady life.
3 Sudden riches.
4 Fatal extravagance.
5 Lucky venture into trade.
6 Sudden fall, great rise.

Love
1 Many lovers.
2 One sincere lover, one false one.
3 A mere flirtation.
4 A fickle illusion.
5 A lover lacking courage to speak.
6 You love but are not loved, break it off.

Courtship
1 The lover is sincere.
2 No marriage is intended.
3 Ambivalence.
4 A long courtship ends in nothing.
5 Ends in marriage.
6 A sudden ending.

Marriage
1 Happy, of long duration.
2 Short, but prosperous and peaceful.
3 Delayed, but happy.
4 Does not end as well as the beginning promised.
5 Separation or divorce.
6 Blissful union.

Children
1 A large and happy brood.
2 Several in number, some roses, others thorns.
3 One at most.
4 Not many.
5 One will bring you wealth, all are loved.
6 Children born outside marriage may prove troublesome.

Family
1 It will enrich you.
2 It will impoverish you.
3 They support you.
4 A dysfunctional family hinders.
5 A valuable inheritance to come.
6 A death in the family.

Commerce
1 No indebtedness.
2 A sudden entry into trade.
3 Friendship with a trader.
4 You will lose through trade.
5 You will enter into partnership.
6 You will make your fortune.

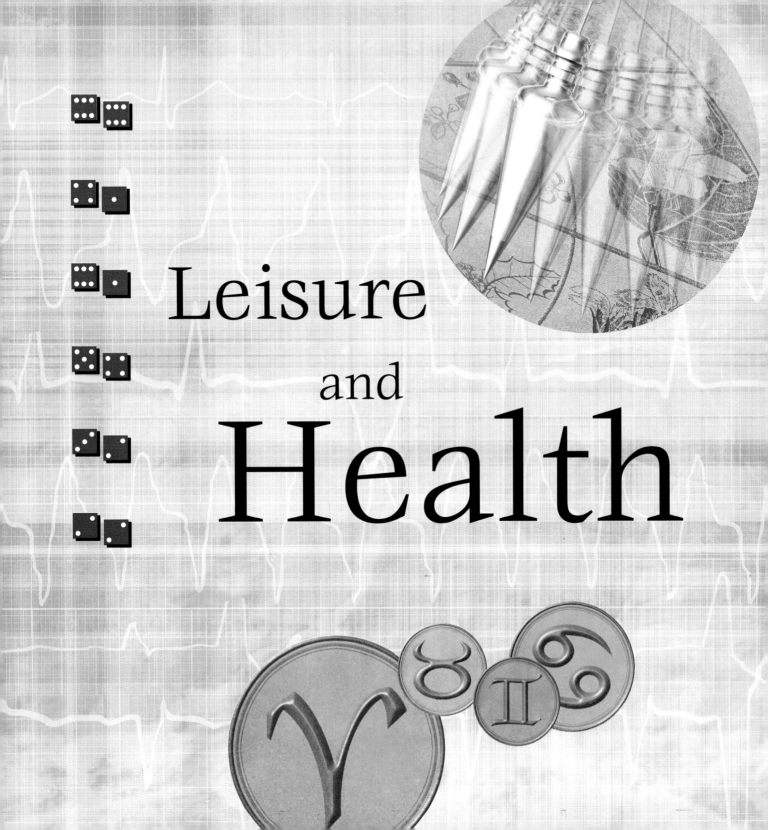

Leisure
and
Health

What to do in our free time and whether we'll remain sufficiently healthy to do all the things we'd like are important for all of us. Leisure will probably become increasingly significant as the twenty-first century unfolds. New possibilities are opening all the time. Many of the ancient oracles can help you decide how to spend your leisure time most profitably. They can also identify hobbies that can be turned into profitable careers.

People often seek guidance as to where to go on vacation — which places will be compatible with their energies. Astrology has many geographical affinities. Use its power to find congenial places and companions. It also can help you to decide whether to go on retreat or to take an evening class in your favorite subject.

Health has always been of concern to questioners and many methods of divination, such as Palmistry for health and medical Astrology, evolved specifically to advise on health matters. They are based on hundreds of years of observation and they can be useful indicators of matters you should take to a physician. Techniques such as Body Dowsing, while not a substitute for medical treatment, identify problems such as stress and nutritional imbalances and help you to select a solution.

Where is it?

Where is the lost item?
Where has s/he gone?
Where's the right place?

It might not always be addressed to oracles, but one of the most frequently asked questions of all is "Where is …?" You might be referring to lost or misplaced items or people, or trying to find an ideal location. Some oracles can tell you if you will find what is missing, and Nine Star Ki can offer favorable directions in which to look, but only Pendulum Dowsing can say exactly where.

Pendulum Dowsing

When you have mastered the art of using a pendulum (see opposite), it is a simple matter to dowse over a map or plan to find lost items or people, or to look for some spot that suits your needs — either professionally or for personal reasons (a favorable place for a move, a career, vacation or a permanent home).

To find lost items, ask the pendulum whether the lost item is in the house, car, garden, office, or wherever you suspect you lost it. Then ask about specific places such as the kitchen, the dining room, etc. Stand where indicated and turn slowly around asking the pendulum to indicate direction. It should lead you directly there. You also can use a map or plan; simply hold the pendulum over the plan and move your finger slowly around the plan. The pendulum will change to a "yes" swing when it is on the spot.

Nine Star Ki

The cyclical nature of this Japanese astrological system means that every year certain directions only will be fortunate ones for you. These are the directions in which you should look for missing items or persons or to which you should look for ideal places for traveling or vacations. The chart on page 184 sets out the favorable directions for the next ten years.

You will first need to know your Nine Star Ki Number. Refer to the chart on page 183. If, for example, you were born in 1969 on or after February 4, you are a 4. If, however, you were born in the same year but between January 1 and February 4, you are a 5.

Pendulum Dowsing

No one is quite sure exactly how dowsing works. It is probable that it picks up minute electrical signals and translates them into imperceptible hand movements that drive a pendulum — one that you've bought or a small object that you've placed on a chain or a piece of cord.

Method

To hold your pendulum: grasp the chain or cord between your thumb and finger with about six inches hanging down with the pendulum at the bottom. You now need to program your pendulum to indicate "yes" and "no." Swing it diagonally in front of you saying "This is yes" a few times. Then swing it diagonally in the opposite direction and say "This is no." Check it out: state your name and ask the pendulum "Is this my name?" It should then show "yes." Say some other name and ask the same question. It should then say "no."

Once you have programmed your pendulum to show "yes" and "no," you can use it in a wide range of applications — choosing a vacation spot or supplements or remedies (see pages 170–1) or to test for allergies that might be making you ill, as below.

If you are trying to identify the source of an allergy, for example, work in a clockwise direction, with the suspected allergens (dairy products and wheat are most common) you want to test laid out in front of you. Put one finger on each item in turn. Hold your pendulum in your other hand and ask "Is this bad for me at this time?". If the answer is "no" move on to the next. If it is "yes," keep checking in case there is more than one item contributing to your ill health.

When should I take a vacation?

Is this a good time for me to take a sabbatical?

Is it time to go on a retreat?

Everyone likes some rest and relaxation and an oracle is often consulted on when is a good time to go. Astrology can pinpoint appropriate times for different types of activities and Fortunate Days also can tell you if this is a good time or not.

Western Astrology

The third house in your birthchart relates to when you make short journeys and its opposite house, the ninth, to longer trips. If either Jupiter or Venus are visiting these houses, it's a good time to take a fun-packed holiday. Romantic Venus would suggest taking a companion along!

If your question is about making a retreat, then look at the eighth house in your birthchart. It is the house of deep introspection and higher consciousness. The ninth house is the religious house of the chart. If either Jupiter or Saturn are affecting these houses, then it would be a good time to withdraw from the world. The ninth house would be a traditional retreat, the eighth house a more "new age" way of doing things.

If you know your birthchart, you can refer to the third, eighth, or ninth house. If not, count your Sun sign as number 1 and count counterclockwise to find the signs for these houses. Check the Astrological Tables (see pages 185–188), to determine when Jupiter, Venus, or Saturn are active there.

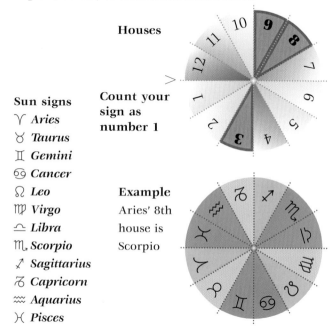

Houses

Sun signs

♈ *Aries*
♉ *Taurus*
♊ *Gemini*
♋ *Cancer*
♌ *Leo*
♍ *Virgo*
♎ *Libra*
♏ *Scorpio*
♐ *Sagittarius*
♑ *Capricorn*
♒ *Aquarius*
♓ *Pisces*

Count your sign as number 1

Example
Aries' 8th house is Scorpio

Fortunate Days

This comprehensive system uses a combination of numerology and astrology to determine days that are good or bad for various activities. You add up the digits of your birthdate to come up with a single-digit number, your Birthdate Number, then you add the digits of the date in question to come up with the Day Number and, finally, you check to see on what day of the week you want to travel. So, for example, if your Birth Number is 6 and the Day Number is 5 and this falls on a Tuesday, the advice shown on the following pages is for you to take a vacation!

Fortunate Days

Calendar

1	2	3	4	5	6	7
8	9	10	11	12	13	14
15	16	17	18	19	20	21
22	23	24	25	26	27	28
29	30	31				

In this system, every number has its own unique vibration — a vibration that can be applied to both your birthdate and the current date. How these vibratory numbers harmonize or conflict with each other, and interact with days of the week, can bring you good fortune or a warning for the future. A reading obtained from your Birthdate Number, the Day Number and the day of the week will cover the next few days. You can do a reading for today, or a date in the future when a particular event could take place — but you will need to know the day of the week on which that date falls.

Method

To find your Birthdate Number, add together the individual digits of your birth day, month and year.

Example If you were born on February 17, 1968 (02/17/1968) that equals

$$|0|2|1|7|1|9|6|8| \ = \ 34 \ = \ 3+4 \ = \ 7$$

To find the Day Number, add together the individual digits of today's date (or any relevant date).

Example January 1, 2001

$$|0|1|0|1|2|0|0|1| \ = \ 5$$

Finally, determine the day of the week on which the Day Number date falls — Sunday, Monday, Tuesday, etc.

In the tables that follow, you will find Birthdate Numbers from 1 to 9 with the Day Number below. To receive advice from the oracle, simply identify your own Birthdate Number, the Day Number of the date you are interested in, and then look up the day on which that date falls.

Birthdate Number 1

Day Number 1

Sunday Immediate prospects excellent. Switch tactics to get around arguments.

Monday Attend to routine, minor matters and correspondence.

Tuesday Go all out after what you want before someone else does.

Wednesday Improve business and social contacts. Inspire confidence in others.

Thursday Act on well-laid plans, otherwise wait. Avoid emotional decisions.

Friday What you start today grows. Push worthwhile projects.

Saturday Further personal ambition not ego. Let others appraise true worth.

Day Number 2

Sunday Don't hesitate or plans spoilt. Act now or efforts wasted.

Monday Don't listen to others or be influenced by rumors. Act on own judgment.

Tuesday Seek advice before making decisions. Return favors.

Wednesday Avoid taking sides or changing plans; people misunderstand or misquote you.

Thursday Seek new friends or source things that you need. Worthwhile plans succeed.

Friday Put ambitions on hold. Help others gain ambition. Be good loser.

Saturday Seek good advice as success hinges on decision made now. Go for it.

Day Number 3

Sunday Try something new, persevere. Trip clears mind for rapid action.

Monday Offer friends help they need. They show lasting appreciation.

Tuesday Work with others as eager for results as you. Exchange of ideas opens new possibilities.

Wednesday Stay with present aims even though badly frustrated. Someone recognizes your abilities and helps.

Thursday Make sure you are going in right direction. Aim too easily gained may spoil something better.

Friday Develop and display talent. Pick work and surroundings best suited to capabilities.

Saturday More you try to figure out what to do, more undecided you become. Wait.

Day Number 4

Sunday Work in harmony, avoid friction. Things go better.

Monday Don't brood over small matters. Perform routine work cheerfully.

Tuesday Do what you do today well as it has important consequences. Don't be diverted from purpose.

Wednesday Advancement certain if you diversify and attend to present projects.

Thursday Use new opportunity in familiar field to advantage. Change of scene boosts energy.

Friday Don't be worn down by present worries. Wishful thinking leads to futile future.

Saturday Put plan into operation before you talk about it or someone will beat you to it.

Day Number 5

Sunday Action and excitement best tonic against depression. Go out and have fun.

Monday More enterprising, more chance of success. Rely on own judgment when taking up something new.

Tuesday New experience is step toward ambition. Good day to take chances and demand what is due.

Wednesday Time to face issues. If avoiding friends or obligations, meet now.

Thursday Whatever you do today, you regret. Avoid anything that brings worries.

Friday Present interests cause you to neglect someone who cares. Give time to romance or friendship.

Saturday Speculative project proves profitable; devote time to it. Make sure you get your share.

Day Number 6

Sunday Day to win friends and influence people, particularly those who aid you. Act conservatively. Be optimistic.

Monday Contact friends you haven't seen in a while. News surprises and leads to something bigger.

Tuesday Do not be distracted from immediate purpose. Be cordial but uncommitted with friends and keep ideas to yourself.

Wednesday Plans upset by events beyond control. Avoid conflicting interests until you decide which one to follow.

Thursday Watch out for false friends who seek to block you to their own advantage.

Friday The more you propose, the more others demand you produce. Do it your way.

Saturday If free from financial risk, be with others who have new ideas and enjoy life. If not, be on your own.

Day Number 7

Sunday Course of intensive study is step to a great future.

Monday Don't let setbacks worry you. Shake off despondency. Smoother path awaits.

Tuesday Weigh decisions to find balance between work and relaxation. Seek culture.

Wednesday Bring yourself up to date on what you plan. Danger of depending on limited knowledge or opinions.

Thursday Hard work cures present problems. Forget past. Think ahead. Results pile up.

Friday Beware clever schemes to defraud you.

Saturday Immediate results on intellectual plane. Business, romance and friendships hinge on meeting of minds.

Day Number 8

Sunday Present plans bring big financial rewards. Don't let anyone talk you out of them.

Monday Bigger hopes, but could be blasted. If someone turns you down, forget it and start over.

Tuesday Today's developments disappoint as too many people involved. Be glad of whatever comes your way.

Wednesday Competition too strong to overcome. Don't be discouraged; experience is profitable.

Thursday Luck, rather than hard work, brings financial rewards or advancement. Something you own gains value.

Friday Watch expenditure. Money wasted cultivating contacts who mean little and care less.

Saturday You may be too trusting. Sign nothing and investigate before investing.

Day Number 9

Sunday Time for self-appraisal. Correct what you have been doing wrong: gain popularity.

Monday More you are seen and heard, happier you become. Make most of artistic urges.

Tuesday Avoid doing favors simply to win popularity, it rebounds. Be blunt with refusals; friends understand.

Wednesday Pass up anything but guaranteed offers. Travel is to advantage but don't chase rainbows.

Thursday Don't criticize those in authority. Their plans are better, so go along with them.

Friday Banish gloom by cheering up friends. They help to solve your worries.

Saturday Popularity is quickest way to profit and achievement. Capitalize on past efforts by bringing to attention of right people.

Birth Number 2

Day Number 1

Sunday Plans need hard work so get started. Further ahead you get, the better.

Monday Don't let present problems worry you. Letter, phone call, or chance meeting provides answer to dilemma.

Tuesday Course you are taking needs approval from friends, so check to avoid disappointment later.

Wednesday You might be mistaken concerning important matters. Check carefully before next step.

Thursday Too many things have been put off. Drop the unimportant, concentrate on rest, especially money.

Friday Offer advice to friends, but don't insist they take it. That way, you are right whatever happens.

Saturday Matters decide themselves due to sudden change in circumstances.

Day Number 2

Sunday Heart-to-heart talk produces lasting happiness through mutual understanding.

Monday Don't mention to anyone anything you are uncertain about. People could exaggerate and blame you.

Tuesday Look for bright side of things. Gloomy outlook spoils happiness.

Wednesday Good day for decisions regarding business or finance. Avoid impulsive spending; try before you buy.

Thursday Other people are making decisions. Have answers ready.

Friday Tell people what they want to hear, make them happy. But don't expect quick answer.

Saturday Argumentative day. Disputes arise between associates that only an outsider can answer.

Day Number 3

Sunday Put talents to good use. Be yourself and others will like you.

Monday Shake off discouragement, concentrate on what lies ahead. Study unfamiliar facts.

Tuesday Audit talents so effort goes into profitable fields.

Wednesday Combine good judgment, capability, and willingness to work for prompt results.

Thursday Several courses open, all attractive but different. Take what offers most.

Friday Pay attention to obligations. Break off association that causes you to forget old friends.

Saturday Be tactful. Conflict of interest threatens romantic and financial welfare. Final decision is due soon.

Day Number 4

Sunday Do not put important things off or difficulties increase and cause despair.

Monday Bad time to risk new ventures. Work hard at what is closest and watch for opportunities there.

Tuesday Near past holds key to present difficulties. Still time to reverse bad decision and regain confidence.

Wednesday If desires unfulfilled, hard work gives answer to pressing problem. First thought should be own welfare.

Thursday More doubts keep you from immediate tasks, stronger they become. Delegate.

Friday Avoid giving advice or taking on new responsibilities or suffer setback.

Saturday Someone plotting to turn your efforts to their advantage, complete present projects quickly.

Day Number 5

Sunday Shake off restraints and take chance. Luck not effort pays off.

Monday Trying times ahead. Stay with bad situation and deal with issues to salvage lost hopes.

Tuesday Keep friendship and finance apart. Take chances with own money or plans, but noone else's.

Wednesday Avoid opinionated people and don't let anyone advise as you could make bad decision. Trips disappointing.

Thursday Getting more deeply involved, particularly in speculation or romance, sees you through.

Friday Wild notions or adventurous weekend prove disastrous. If daydreaming, let it drop.

Saturday Pile one adventure on another. Plan well, then go, go, go.

Day Number 6

Sunday Make choice, seek support of reliable friends; results may surprise.

Monday If others need help, try "I'll scratch your back, you scratch mine."

Tuesday Be guided by past experience. Don't let other people sway you.

Wednesday Prove to others you can finish what you started, and deliver.

Thursday You have to work at popularity, other people want things from you.

Friday Big surprise. Extra duty upon you opens new opportunities.

Saturday Wonderful weekend. Play social contacts to full.

Day Number 7

Sunday Lack of recognition makes you dissatisfied. Drop outside interests and concentrate on what you do best.

Monday Avoid starting anything new today. Study or self-improvement helps cope with what is coming.

Tuesday Treat everything lightly today. Postpone romantic decisions.

Wednesday What you have undertaken needs extra work.

Thursday Trouble threatens; retreat quickly and wait for it to pass.

Friday Resolve misunderstandings with regard to business, pleasure, or love.

Saturday Examine ambitions carefully. Avoid depressing people; accept advice from those who can help.

Day Number 8

Sunday Try to get people on your side rather than going against them.

Monday Make firm decision and follow through for personal gain. Good timing important.

Tuesday Opportunities may look big now, but prove small. Pass up.

Wednesday Swapping old for new brings profitable surprise.

Thursday Careful planning and correct advice turns current problems into profit or advancement.

Friday Plans you think solid vanish with wind unless contingency plans ready.

Saturday Completion of immediate aims leads to something bigger, but avoid legal entanglements and dubious promises.

Day Number 9

Sunday Concentrate on big ambition only as long as even partial success brings recognition.

Monday Day for going around in circles. Honor may be worthless; think over carefully.

Tuesday Big promises mean nothing. False friends deceive. Obligations heavy, luck pulls through.

Wednesday Social events of great value; attend whatever you can. Count on old friends but make new ones, too.

Thursday Avoid restlessness and impatience. People may believe you take advantage.

Friday Build up goodwill by freely helping neighborhood. Substantial return results.

Saturday Make sure you can cope before accepting important office or duty. Failure a great setback.

Birth Number 3

Day Number 1

Sunday Expand activities rather than concentrating on one.

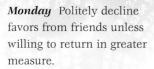

Monday Politely decline favors from friends unless willing to return in greater measure.

Tuesday Friction over minor matters could ruin immediate hopes. Go along with other people, but reserve judgment.

Wednesday If you suspect others of plotting against you, you are probably right, but keep it to yourself.

Thursday Too much talk spoils plans. Focus mind on what you want and it comes your way.

Friday Look back to the past week to see what opportunities were missed. Catch up on a few over the weekend.

Saturday Put all your eggs in one basket, but keep an eye on the basket! Don't let anyone take what is rightfully yours.

Day Number 2

Sunday Get what you want by following established rules but don't impose them on others.

Monday In conflicts of interest, do not compromise, go one way or other.

Tuesday Intentions may be suspected or challenged by someone as strong as you. If you can't beat them, join them.

Wednesday Develop what you started without short cuts to fame and fortune. Budding romance could flare into passion.

Thursday Present plans profitable if you rely on own efforts. If new friends have not proved worth, break off.

Friday Think twice before proceeding with new plans. Your suggestions might be resented, keep calm if criticized.

Saturday Time to turn dreams into reality. Go where need is greatest and gear work to popular demand.

Day Number 3

Sunday Going to extremes may prove undoing. If you can't concentrate on one thing, eliminate ones that cause most worry.

Monday Any deal coming up needs full attention as minor matters could ruin great opportunity.

Tuesday Plan carefully, itemize aims and see each through as neglect could mean failure.

Wednesday Someone trying to use your brains for own advantage. Switch plans to circumvent.

Thursday Don't force ideas on others. Follow own inclinations and ask their opinion later when they cannot back out.

Friday What you start today brings good results. Take advantage of vitality now.

Saturday Stop wasting time on things that you like but are not worth the effort. More gain elsewhere.

Day Number 4

Sunday Slow down, work hard at what promises most returns, and await results.

Monday Don't let routine work irritate. Once colleagues recognize your worth, bigger things follow.

Tuesday Keep quiet about present plans; complete before another moves in on you. Jealousy in air.

Wednesday Be independent. Go where action is, friends back you in arguments.

Thursday New friends help toward quick success. Enjoy yourself but don't neglect important work.

Friday Caution needed in new ventures. Someone trying to outdo you? If one method fails, use another.

Saturday Do not antagonize anyone this weekend. Business or pleasure trip forestalls a difficult decision.

Day Number 5

Sunday Excellent day for going places and making new friends. Bold, decisive action brings popularity.

Monday Expand activities and try out new ideas; use your initiative to full.

Tuesday Travel brings profit and pleasure: are you missing bigger pleasure at home? Someone taking advantage.

Wednesday Don't let flattering offers tempt you away from present prospects. Seek friends' advice.

Thursday Do whatever you plan alone or someone else takes credit.

Friday Plan travel or personal contacts to expand viewpoint. Success in new and untried fields.

Saturday Include friends or family on a trip. Avoid impulsive action.

Day Number 6

Sunday End financial worry by eliminating unnecessary social activities. Budget for economy.

Monday Overemphasis on personal desires could prove disastrous to business or personal life. Allocate time to each.

Tuesday Work in harmony, compliment those around you. Ask for advice.

Wednesday Give thought to small ideas as well as big ones, especially at home.

Thursday Hold back impulse for something new. Ask advice before dropping established work.

Friday If too contented, miss opportunities. Seek them out.

Saturday Time to repay social obligations and pave way for new. Remain optimistic.

Day Number 7

Sunday Take time for yourself. Consider what lies ahead. Avoid decisions and ignore advice until you see what develops.

Monday Don't let worries drag you down. If something wrong, new approach will solve it.

Tuesday Good ideas that need developing. Get busy on this now.

Wednesday Expand efforts and turn inspiration into reality. Don't waste time on wrong people.

Thursday Don't criticize what others have to say. Listening brings ideas for own use.

Friday Stop planning and start doing. Think back to something practical and take off from there.

Saturday Keep mind on creative endeavors over weekend. You have abilities; don't waste them.

Day Number 8

Sunday Keep own counsel or friends will appropriate your ideas.

Monday Original ideas in business pay off if you work out details. Accept helpful suggestions.

Tuesday Don't be impatient with people who fall short. Help wins loyalty you might need.

Wednesday Don't let outsiders or gossip upset home life.

Thursday If things go smoothly, you could be object of envy. Confide in long-standing friends only.

Friday Build on business gains. Diversify interests and follow through what pans out best.

Saturday Start building name and reputation. People will come to you.

Day Number 9

Sunday Don't accept honors that mean work rather than prestige. Pass to others; wait for something better.

Monday Finish task at hand before you begin another. You make a better choice.

Tuesday Family welfare or community projects may need a hand. Gain real prestige.

Wednesday Don't let minor problems distract from major goal. Bigger you think, smaller obstacles become.

Thursday Ability and popularity brings joint profits. Good time to merge interests.

Friday Over-ambition sends you toward futile goal. Sound out those who oppose you, then decide.

Saturday Quiet persistence rather than assertion wins others to your side.

Birth Number 4

Day Number 1

Sunday Plan methodical study routine. Do not expect immediate results; cooperation comes from others.

Monday Forget worries. Establish confidence in those around you and succeed.

Tuesday You may prefer to act slowly but quick decision is important.

Wednesday Do not run away from problems; recognition then goes far beyond hopes.

Thursday If working for others, do something for yourself. Calling on others shows true friends.

Friday Stop vacillating and get on with it.

Saturday New fields open quickly; choose a goal and be confident in own ability.

Day Number 2

Sunday Plans for today may fade through disinterest. Prepare for future problems instead.

Monday Good time to follow natural inclinations and take advantage of opportunities. Let others set pace.

Tuesday Friends and associates give you what you need; do not antagonize them.

Wednesday Concentrate on purpose not results. Avoid rash business decisions.

Thursday Avoid big things, you wear yourself out and meet opposition. Good for detail.

Friday Excellent for contracts and cooperative effort.

Saturday Catch up on neglected correspondence, renew old acquaintances, future opportunities develop.

Day Number 3

Sunday Deal with correspondence, detail, obligations, and piled-up data.

Monday Active period, plenty of opportunity. Hunches pay off.

Tuesday Avoid rash business decisions and do not pressure others.

Wednesday Discuss new projects or proper handling of old ones. Check legal matters, contracts.

Thursday Sound out friends as they may give you what you need. If no response, drop it.

Friday Survey minor problems and plan new projects with associates.

Saturday Start early as day brings changes and opportunities.

Day Number 4

Sunday Embark on projects to help others. Seek harmony and inspiration.

Monday Apply skills to increasing production and funds. Guard health.

Tuesday Avoid unprofitable tasks. Good for concentrated, productive work.

Wednesday Devote time to social or public events that bring in cash.

Thursday Work hard with others who share your drive.

Friday Plan future events; combine social and business interests.

Saturday Strictly a day for socializing.

Day Number 5

Sunday Use own initiative, avoid advice, big opportunities follow soon.

Monday Beware; people might use your efforts for their gain.

Tuesday Develop your social talents, which gain you more than hard work.

Wednesday Do things yourself; relying on promises brings disaster.

Thursday Keep doing what you are doing; luck comes in surprising way.

Friday Friendship is keynote today. Further it.

Saturday Look back on accomplishments and strive to improve with less effort.

Day Number 6

Sunday Peace of mind and security are your reward if you don't let obstacles get in the way of ambition.

Monday Renew old acquaintances. Friends and family help to fulfill a wish.

Tuesday Trying day, keep cool. Avoid arguments as they cause pain later.

Wednesday Difficult day, try another angle later but avoid indecision.

Thursday Seek out people in education fields and embrace their philosophy. Good day for public events.

Friday Everyone has problems and yours will pass in due time. Avoid instability.

Saturday Excellent day for promoting your abilities. Develop and use your talents to gain success.

Day Number 7

Sunday Enjoy friends and family.

Monday Think before you leap; there may be much work ahead.

Tuesday Initiative brings success. Decide, then get things moving.

Wednesday Social contacts useful for promoting plans and raising money. Presentation important.

Thursday Responsibilities seem lighter if you remain receptive. Avoid gloom.

Friday Beware sharp practice in business deal or purchase. Look at details.

Saturday Try new venture beyond your expectations. Good for money.

Day Number 8

Sunday Avoid change that affects financial status. Better to stay put than lose money on gamble.

Monday Look for unexpected. New undertaking could benefit financially.

Tuesday Cheerfulness pays off in time and money.

Wednesday Avoid criticizing. Work harder to maintain position.

Thursday Plan for future ambition. Protect against loss.

Friday Follow own ideas but plan each step carefully.

Saturday Do something creative; research, study. Avoid impatience.

Day Number 9

Sunday Plan long-range project or qualifications: give it your full attention.

Monday Weigh plans, reserve decisions. Stay with what you're doing and problems resolve.

Tuesday Whatever you do you'll wish you'd done something else, but it would have been worse.

Wednesday Trying for fast results creates setbacks.

Thursday Go all out for big ideas backed by others.

Friday Establish yourself with family and friends; improve homelife.

Saturday Think of yourself for a change. Decide how to get more out of life.

Birth Number 5

Day Number 1

Sunday You may not like to conform, but harmonize originality with others.

Monday Weigh all knowledge acquired. Use drive and initiative.

Tuesday Make most of opportunities but do not overlook work at hand and advice from superiors.

Wednesday Do not let enthusiasm become aggressive.

Thursday Study everything for immediate not future possibilities. Good prospects.

Friday Deal with correspondence. Dependability brings rewards.

Saturday Go along with those in power. Be forceful, analyze.

Day Number 2

Sunday Proceed with personal goals but do not conflict with people close to you.

Monday Budget for new schemes.

Tuesday Concentrate on own talents; select single slant to reflect versatility.

Wednesday Impulse can be costly, constant efforts pay off; investigate science.

Thursday Avoid chances and unnecessary debts.

Friday Avoid idle chitchat. Create confidence in people for success.

Saturday Combine studiousness with practical abilities to increase finances.

Day Number 3

Sunday Check finances, ensure future. Enjoy yourself, but provide for needs.

Monday Maintain harmony with others despite work problems.

Tuesday Use good counsel to help others and keep harmony among friends.

Wednesday Don't let restlessness spoil opportunities. Routine duties require patience.

Thursday Seek advice regarding money matters. Seek new methods of advancement.

Friday You may want new surroundings, but hold onto work and security.

Saturday Good day for love, family, friendship.

Day Number 4

Sunday Trying day. Use diplomacy to avoid friction; leave complications to others.

Monday Altercations with those near you. If you can't help, don't interfere.

Tuesday Carefully consider new venture or employment.

Wednesday Propitious day for anything new regarding occupation. Consult others about fresh ideas.

Thursday Accept love of someone close. Happiness shared makes things brighter.

Friday Be careful when traveling. Impulsiveness leads to unexpected.

Saturday Consider personal needs and resolve to be kinder to yourself.

Day Number 5

Sunday Make contact with friends.

Monday Work harder; whatever the project, you benefit.

Tuesday Take time over decisions, maintain own viewpoint.

Wednesday Plan for next month. Find new interest that adds to income.

Thursday Change tactics. More happiness and less friction if you avoid certain people.

Friday Talk to friend. Love helps the lonely.

Saturday Learn truth rather than gossip before forming negative opinion.

Day Number 6

Sunday Don't let jealousy of another upset you.

Monday If you loan money, be sure you have ample security.

Tuesday Refrain from quick decisions.

Wednesday Excellent time for new groups, social activities.

Thursday Clear up loose ends. Try new project.

Friday Let others know what you need. Ask for assistance or financial cooperation.

Saturday Stay within own circle. Study and contemplate.

Day Number 7

Sunday Start early to keep ahead. Don't spend more than you can afford.

Monday Consult and cooperate with others. Thrift better than extravagance.

Tuesday Visit close friends or family, or help community.

Wednesday Avoid escapism; stay where you are. Good news soon.

Thursday Take care of personal business. Don't let dissension deter.

Friday Great time for love or recreation. Give attention to someone vital.

Saturday Look after finances; plan for years ahead. Protect savings. Do not tolerate interference.

Day Number 8

Sunday Enjoy whatever presents itself. Family comes first.

Monday Maintain conservative attitude. Refrain from arguments. Digression harms.

Tuesday Entanglements may upset; try to be constructive. Eat wisely, take care of health.

Wednesday Good financial period approaches. Tempting offers; beware sharp practice.

Thursday Be patient. Change of location or old relationship could alter circumstances.

Friday Clever thinking puts you ahead, improves living conditions.

Saturday Coordinate ideas with other people for mutual benefit. Relax.

Day Number 9

Sunday Self-reliance pays off. Avoid distracting friction.

Monday Keep opinions to yourself; someone could betray trust.

Tuesday Be creative, pursue goals, but have fun.

Wednesday Good day for new ideas. Leave arrogance to others.

Thursday Enthusiasm and experience bring opportunity. Get credit if needed.

Friday Dependability offsets criticism. Let nothing disturb efficiency.

Saturday Stay with routine chores and personal business; solve complex problems.

Birth Number 6

Day Number 1

Sunday Give attention to opportunities close to home; results surprise.

Monday Go along with others even if you disagree on small points. They'll come around.

Tuesday Check out rumors of someone else seeking a reward that should be yours.

Wednesday If opposing parties try to woo you, don't give in too soon. Things turn about.

Thursday Romance and travel just around the corner.

Friday Drop people who depend on your good nature to shoulder burdens.

Saturday Go along on trip proposed by friends or family.

Day Number 2

Sunday Don't let sympathies waver during coming week or lose prestige.

Monday Plan for brief but complete change.

Tuesday Stop crossing bridges before you get there, most problems imaginary, rest cancel out.

Wednesday Watch others, then act.

Thursday Ignore well-intentioned advice; put work first.

Friday Don't try to convince people you can put across new ideas. Prove it.

Saturday When weighing up inducements to go elsewhere, remember there's no place like home.

Day Number 3

Sunday New project beneficial if using past experience and present capability.

Monday Don't sacrifice talents through fear of insecurity. Get advice on adjusting to more profitable circumstances.

Tuesday Excellent artistic, literary, inventive prospects if contacting right people.

Wednesday Put aside social contacts and hobbies until sure of better job.

Thursday Chance to appear on TV, or gain election to office; could disrupt well-set plans.

Friday Avoid complacency and self-sufficiency; cultivate friends who shake you out of them.

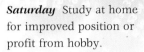

Saturday Study at home for improved position or profit from hobby.

Day Number 4

Sunday Stop wasting time on detail; decide what is essential for coming week. Results amaze.

Monday Pay more attention to home life. Read instructive books.

Tuesday For immediate gain, put existing plans into action instead of talking.

Wednesday Overgenerous, others benefit from your efforts. Think of yourself.

Thursday Going round in large circle? Make it smaller and get back to earth.

Friday Work you like and what you have to do runs you ragged. Slow up, let people appreciate you.

Saturday Gain from own efforts increased by family funds or business venture.

Day Number 5

Sunday Personal problems cause business worries. Choose or lose out.

Monday Put affairs in order before taking on new projects or long trip.

Tuesday Take vacation; visit old friends.

Wednesday Stop yearning to be something different. Keep home fires burning or they may go out.

Thursday Unexpected recognition due. How much depends on factors involved.

Friday Don't let anyone hinder drive for success. When at top, solve their problems easily.

Saturday Dismiss past regrets. New contracts/projects promise rapid success if past experience used to advantage.

Day Number 6

Sunday Handicrafts bring profit if you persevere.

Monday New experiences promise gain, especially if travel involved. Use linguistic abilities. Follow social inclinations.

Tuesday Important invitation or offer in near future is stepping stone to something bigger.

Wednesday New opportunities from study or special training; consider offers and contracts carefully.

Thursday Friends or relatives give new outlook on business or profession. Act on advice but don't bank on promises.

Friday Good intuition. Hunches pay off, don't overdo it.

Saturday Long-laid plan or cherished hope ready for fulfillment. Letter, call, or news item important.

Day Number 7

Sunday Old friend or adviser snaps you out of intellectual coma with exciting offer. Take it!

Monday If happy where you are, stay. If happy with what you're doing, carry on. Anything else, backward step.

Tuesday Responsibilities hinder artistic or intellectual attainments. Decide what is important and act!

Wednesday Work with those who appreciate abilities. Get your share of success.

Thursday Look closely at associates now.

Friday Settle family problems; finish business deals. Enjoy weekend.

Saturday Beware legal problems. Avoid attractive business deals.

Day Number 8

Sunday Time for happiness. If others agree with you OK; if not, ignore.

Monday Friend or relative may seek advice. Give it; what have you to lose?

Tuesday Whatever you plan succeeds if followed through. Success breeds success.

Wednesday Everything comes your way. News from old friend, offer from new acquaintance, end to family worries.

Thursday Concentrate on own plans for as long as needed.

Friday Domestic and business matters in balance. Let someone else decide.

Saturday Small beginnings grow into great opportunities. Remember old friends.

Day Number 9

Sunday People who did small favors now want large return. Avoid mixing sentiment and generosity.

Monday May be expecting too much too soon. Try new tactics and take time.

Tuesday Broaden activities, make new friends, inspire confidence.

Wednesday Grant friends favors but specify fair return to help new project.

Thursday Divided interests thwart progress. Bring groups together.

Friday Wasting time on what you like rather than what is valuable? Diversify.

Saturday Study all eventualities before deciding goal. More attractive the prospects, harder work to follow.

Birth Number 7

Day Number 1

Sunday Introspection leads to important goal; gear actions to aims.

Monday Put present knowledge to immediate use. Reluctance results in others getting what you should have.

Tuesday Balance forebodings against fresh outlook. Happy companions banish blues.

Wednesday Put thoughts on paper.

Thursday Putting off unpleasant task causes anxiety. Do it or too late.

Friday May have to sacrifice existing plans for new and exciting future. Go for it!

Saturday In harmonious surroundings, surefire success.

Day Number 2

Sunday Don't hold back on big opportunity; go for it. Push plans with people who can help.

Monday Indecision puts you in hopeless mood. Let others decide.

Tuesday Diversify interests. Surprise from unexpected quarter.

Wednesday To ease job or improve business, think what others can do under your direction.

Thursday Too much study, lose interest. Fun with friends surplants troublesome tasks.

Friday Conference with important people shapes future beyond all expectations.

Saturday Turn present experience to broader and more productive fields. Short trip helps.

Day Number 3

Sunday Aggressive period, emotional upsets. Avoid complications; rest.

Monday Solve difficult situations for others; your prospects improve.

Tuesday Limit social activities. Concentrate on tasks that need your complete attention.

Wednesday Formative and changeable period. Meetings broaden outlook.

Thursday Overwork demands rest. Concentrate on work; it pays dividends.

Friday Conserve energy. Don't let associates intrude. Follow intuition socially.

Saturday Use good judgment and proceed with aims and ambitions. Good for advancement.

Day Number 4

Sunday Use knowledge to improve situation. Curb extravagance. Friends support.

Monday Early morning luck. Important tasks await.

Tuesday Help those who need you but don't get involved in personal upsets; own needs come first.

Wednesday Business outlook very favorable. Let others know and support plans.

Thursday Venture into new area where talent can expand. Use initiative to get results.

Friday Exercise patience. Look for ways to increase financial gain.

Saturday Mutual money matters take upward turn. Have fun close to home.

Day Number 5

Sunday Unexpected opportunity to travel or broaden activities may result in intensive work. Weigh prospects carefully.

Monday Surprises are coming your way. Don't be alarmed, all will be well.

Tuesday Be cautious in business deals now; someone wants your ideas.

Wednesday Change due in your affairs or those of associates. Adjust to new circumstances.

Thursday Changing your opinion brings specific benefits.

Friday Quick solution to personal problems through trusted friend.

Saturday Neglected purpose should be pursued now. Good results from special effort.

Day Number 6

Sunday Give mental efforts practical application. Turn knowledge into cash.

Monday Pay attention to home life -- results good.

Tuesday Problems become magnified in mind. Eliminate until one remains. Concentrate on that.

Wednesday Bigger ideas, bigger chance of success. Test on others; watch reactions.

Thursday Far ahead of your time, wait for others to catch up. Stay with what you're doing.

Friday Be direct in everything. Ask favors. Aim for something bigger or better.

Saturday Let people ask for what they want. They give to you in return.

Day Number 7

Sunday Quiet and harmony needed for progress. Work alone and tell no one until completed.

Monday Possibility of planning too far ahead or on too big scale. Seek practical partner or sponsor.

Tuesday Discount worries or obstacles; on verge of big success.

Wednesday Devote time to intellectual pursuits. Read books or attend lectures.

Thursday Check knowledge of subject before embarking on project. May need updating.

Friday If friends seek advice, snap judgments or set opinions could cause them to blame you if things go wrong.

Saturday New approaches to problems improve position. One avenue fails, try another.

Day Number 8

Sunday Forget self, shower affection on loved ones.

Monday Curb impulsiveness and do not be temperamental. Concentrate on ambitions and business interests.

Tuesday Understanding needed. Coming change needs decisions.

Wednesday No time to be emotional over situation at home. Use common sense. Protect property.

Thursday Conserve energy for problems. Keep assets mobile and secrets to yourself.

Friday Don't let misunderstanding confuse issues. Important decisions need calmness and good judgment.

Saturday Mix with congenial people, develop new ideas, plan for vacation.

Day Number 9

Sunday Time is of essence. Coordinate social and business activities. Try to increase income.

Monday Go along with associates for time being. Finances need boost, keep ambitious schemes under control.

Tuesday Collect what is due. Accept hospitality offered by debtors or opponents.

Wednesday Trying period, stay calm. Don't let others know you are worried.

Thursday Responsibilities weigh heavily but must be met. Rewards later.

Friday Give service despite sense of inferiority; you will be winner.

Saturday Intuition or events bring change of mind. Make new plans if necessary.

Birth Number 8

Day Number 1

Sunday Able to help others, do not be affected by their depression. Have fun.

Monday Do not go to extremes with generosity. Domestic irritation irks, do not add to problems.

Tuesday Check veracity of salesmen before investing. Stay close to home.

Wednesday Expedite working practices. Make sure accounts in order. Talk with others improves your interests.

Thursday Relax and enjoy yourself in good company. Problems find solutions.

Friday Solve problems and reconcile accounts in morning. Spend rest of day with congenial friends.

Saturday Solitude brings excellent results. Study and peruse important documents.

Day Number 2

Sunday If friends upset you, dismiss it. Demonstrate initiative and ability.

Monday Avoid parental or domestic boredom. Maintain silence and patience. Look to career or personal interest.

Tuesday Do nothing to upset basic security. Lend hand to needy. Look after health.

Wednesday Loved one may not understand financial arrangements; continue good management.

Thursday Emotional time due to friction and gossip, do not let this deter you from work.

Friday Do not waiver in faith or decisions regarding work or personal matters. Accept change.

Saturday Personal, social, or business achievement. Avoid grumblers.

Day Number 3

Sunday Help someone you neither know nor care for. Rest and study.

Monday Check property and possessions. Be tactful. Budget carefully.

Tuesday Listen to friends and colleagues. Do not digress from objectives.

Wednesday News may be to your advantage. Maintain perspective on plans.

Thursday Irritability makes matters worse. Avoid people and do not become involved in arguments.

Friday Lock up cash and property. Do not force showdown.

Saturday Occupation is affected by new trend. Help others better their lot.

Day Number 4

Sunday Be cool and calm in crisis. Check everything — carefully.

Monday Avoid emotional reactions with family and friends. Remain firm in convictions despite complications.

Tuesday Look into new opportunities. Important everything you undertake is right for you.

Wednesday Be cheerful. Spend less, save more. Surprise in near future.

Thursday Progress and advancement in business. Time for change.

Friday Worry over complications from past. Be confident and eliminate problem permanently.

Saturday Change of plans due to those around you. Optimism gains what you need most.

Day number 5

Sunday Plan new work ideas. Achieve more with cooperation of friends.

Monday Do not seek help. Concentrate on immediate responsibilities.

Tuesday Capitalize on your abilities, luck is with you. Do not offend anyone.

Wednesday Raise funds for yourself or organization. Check assets if financing self. Accuracy important.

Thursday Start early to accomplish much. Tact and diplomacy aid. Deal with safe enterprises only.

Friday Have some fun. Try something new. Get away. Love important.

Saturday Day for romance and pleasure.

Day Number 6

Sunday Relax, meditate. Relatives and in-laws add to enjoyment.

Monday Cultivate new acquaintances. Increase social activities.

Tuesday Do what you can to improve prestige. Be dignified. Keep witticisms for evening.

Wednesday New impetus in afternoon. Save money; let others pay. Good for sport and entertainment.

Thursday Check health, do not overwork. Avoid discussions of personal problems.

Friday Seek advice from friends but use own judgment. Consider travel and investments.

Saturday Solitude is good; devote time to real opportunities. Avoid family disputes.

Day Number 7

Sunday Look to debit side of expenditure, economy needed. Lunar influence indicates change for better.

Monday Stay with reliable associates, bankers, law firms, and interests. Avoid hypersensitive colleagues.

Tuesday Dependents may irritate but patience rewarded. Favorable period.

Wednesday Follow desires in morning — whatever they are. Rest of day happy despite obstacles.

Thursday Regardless of how high thoughts soar, obligations have to be met.

Friday Make plans early; great satisfaction especially if friend included.

Saturday Day filled with surprises, not all good but mostly happy. Plan unusual excursion.

Day Number 8

Sunday Keep mind on immediate projects. Do not let anything pile up. Pay debts promptly.

Monday Stay with reliable friends, do not upset sensitive ones. Be cautious of ideals.

Tuesday Use patience and analytic ability to ward off complications with family or associates. New events bring happiness.

Wednesday Utilize morning to best advantage. Relaxation important.

Thursday Aim forceful nature toward success. Balance all angles to override opposition.

Friday Put plans and executive ability to work. Inspire loyalty through understanding people.

Saturday Avoid ruthless force. Study people and problems. Indecision passes. Cooperation helps you.

Day Number 9

Sunday Do not waste energies. Use drive for advancement in business or social circles. Be above petty jealousy.

Monday Plan carefully. Capability extends to greatest achievements.

Tuesday Be aggressive; follow trends and move on without resentment.

Wednesday Follow intuition but back with advice from family or friends. Formulate plan before plunging into new venture.

Thursday Thinking big helps where money concerned. Do not waste energy on irrelevant matters. Relax.

Friday Dependability prevalent but don't expect cooperation from others. Good results cumulative.

Saturday Change brings different opinion. Vacation relieves strain.

Birth Number 9

Day Number 1

Sunday Give full attention to immediate occupation. Avoid extravagance. If speculating, do not invest in bad risk.

Monday Act now to demand more for efforts but do not exceed maximum. Others have same to offer.

Tuesday Ability to cope with situation before you. Fruition of efforts in day, week, or month.

Wednesday If you must make changes, take chance but try to retain balance.

Thursday If on verge of decision regarding money, wait until more influential. Act independently.

Friday Put imagination into ideas, play hunches. Take vacation later.

Saturday Use intellect creatively, set goal within capabilities. Cling to ambition but adapt.

Day Number 2

Sunday Cultivate new friendships. Good news ahead but release tension.

Monday Talent great but do not extend beyond capacity.

Tuesday Profitable changes. Do not take easy way out; seek reasonable solution.

Wednesday Fulfill obligations, expect rewards.

Thursday Speculate, change, live up to ideals. Leave drudgery to others.

Friday Devote time to business and home life. If things not as you wish, keep trying.

Saturday Use influence to help those in need. Make best of opportunity.

Day Number 3

Sunday Stay with present routine. Change means disappointment.

Monday Consider future and present security. Keep glamor for holiday.

Tuesday Use versatility to further ends.

Wednesday Study new ideas thoroughly. Be sure all is right before proceeding.

Thursday Initiative is fine but cooperate with others even though not to your liking.

Friday Use own forcefulness to improve conditions. Establish good will and respect.

Saturday Make weekend interesting. Study to increase knowledge.

Day Number 4

Sunday Join friends in fun and excitement. Do not let interests conflict with others.

Monday Take things easier, accomplish more. Compliment those who aid. Honesty and reliability great assets.

Tuesday Plan for distant future. Take advice to gain success at top level. Do not worry about opposition.

Wednesday Work steadily. Treat problems with patience. Stability secret of success.

Thursday Adventurous era but avoid extravagant spending to impress. Celebrate attaining rightful place in world.

Friday Kindliness helps achieve goals, though may face aggression. Do not be disturbed. New vistas good for you.

Saturday Study arts or skill. Try change of pace.

Day Number 5

Sunday Do not listen to gossip. Stay busy, do not give up ambition.

Monday Keep within bounds of own capabilities. Apply sound investment principles.

Tuesday Versatility and intuition aid planning. Proceed.

Wednesday Concentrate on own affairs. Check and fulfill personal needs.

Thursday Put ideas for home or office to work. Avoid procrastination. Travel if you must, but adventure is where you are.

Friday Accomplish something worthwhile. Create confidence, make yourself indispensable.

Saturday Buy no more than you need, even food. Luxury items must wait. Solitude inspires.

Fortunate Days *(continued)*

Day Number 6

Sunday Mix with young people. Analyze problems perceptively. Do not believe all you hear.

Monday Complications lead to conferences. Substantiate every part of argument. Leave antagonism to others. Rely on superior authority.

Tuesday Use originality to help mold your surroundings. Let nothing deter you.

Wednesday If you make financial pact, relationship with associates becomes strained. This costs dearly and alienates friends.

Thursday Confidence in undertakings — go ahead. If not, wait. If angle foreign to you, give long perusal.

Friday Ensure possessions safe and protected. Keep plans to yourself. Do not be discouraged.

Saturday Mystic powers work for you. Keep social activities to minimum.

Day Number 7

Sunday Meet issues head on; use honest approach to solve. Make schedule you can meet. Accept cooperation of others.

Monday Find solace in own pursuits.

Tuesday Evasion is not solution to difficulty. No answer, let associates step in. Rivals produce competitive blocks; unravel.

Wednesday Creative ability places responsibilities on you. Delegate. Take time for home and socializing.

Thursday If making investment, consult someone who knows. Think about further moves.

Friday Small disturbances irksome but finish tasks. Move with discretion.

Saturday Work or relaxation, you hold key to knowledge and can direct new ventures.

Day Number 8

Sunday Promote personal ambition but avoid opinions that could upset advancement.

Monday New contacts valuable. Don't be discouraged.

Tuesday Material success and business important.

Wednesday Try something new but take no chances. Forget routine, meet surprises with delight.

Thursday Use new friendships to further ideals.

Friday Keep family happy, then enlarge and publicize your work interests.

Saturday Devote time to ambitions. Time is of essence. Let friends go who do not aid.

Day Number 9

Sunday Protect home, take stock of business needs. Set house and finances in order.

Monday Propitious time for planning new ventures. Keep social life at home.

Tuesday Let people and press know what you're doing. Aim for honor and distinction. Money follows.

Wednesday May encounter difficulties but influences good. Do not be careless or wasteful.

Thursday Business prospects good. Avoid heavy investments. If artistic, test of ability and initiative.

Friday Plan social get-together. Do not spend more than you can afford.

Saturday Time for fun, relaxation, and romance. Listen while you learn.

Where should I go on vacation?

What type of holiday would be best for me?

Nine Star Ki can pinpoint the direction in which you should travel. Dowsing can direct you to a particular country or area of the country. Your Sun sign will help you to pick the activities and places that are certain to please. Choose the right place for your sign, and you cannot fail to have a good time.

Pendulum Dowsing

You can use a pendulum to find a suitable spot for a holiday once you have programmed your pendulum to show "yes" and "no" (see page 137).
Start with a map of the world. Ask about your own country first; if the answer is "yes" move onto more detailed maps of the country until you find the right area. If the answer is "no," put your finger on other countries until you find the right one. Then use a map of that country to refine the answer. You also can use a pendulum to check out the hotels in a travel brochure.

Nine Star Ki

This Eastern system is based on a nine-year cycle in which, depending on your Nine Star Ki Number, certain directions are more propitious than others in each year. To determine your number, refer to the chart on page 183. If, for example, you were born in 1974 on or after February 4, you are an 8. If, however, you were born between January 1 and February 4 in the same year, you would be a 9. Refer to the chart on page 184 to see which directions will be most favorable. If you are a number 8, for example, then traveling north and east-northeast would be recommended in 2003.

Sun Signs

Certain places have an affinity with Zodiac signs, and the signs all have favorite ways of spending their vacations. Some love to travel — especially the fire and air signs, others like to stay with what is familiar and known — the earth signs, although you can usually tempt Capricorn into mountains. Water signs yearn for watery pursuits and places, they usually dislike planes and opt for ferries. Fire signs fly off for hot sun, sex and sand, or take their cars adventuring. If you are not sure where to go on vacation, let astrology point the way:

Aries

Frenetic activity in a hot place suits sporty Aries. No lying on the beach for you. You are on the move, seeking excitement. Dangerous sports particularly appeal, as does anywhere with a spark of danger.

Places Resorts with sporting facilities. England; Germany; Israel; Burgundy, France; Florence, Naples and Padua, Italy; Krakow, Poland; Las Vegas; and Brunswick.

Taurus

You like somewhere warm, comfortable, and luxurious, with excellent food, and you don't hesitate to pay extra for good service. An indolent sign, you take things easy, preferably in gently rolling countryside.

Places Luxury hotels. Cyprus; Iran; Greek Islands; Turkey; Ireland, especially Dublin; Leipzig, Germany; Mantua, Parma and Palermo, Italy; St. Louis.

Gemini

You get as much enjoyment out of planning your holiday as going away. Cities suit you. Variety and people do it for you. A crowded street, a market, anywhere you can talk.

Places City centers. Armenia; Sardinia; Belgium; USA especially New York and San Francisco; London, England; Lombardy, Italy; Cordoba, Spain; Nuremberg, Germany.

Cancer

You seek somewhere peaceful near water — a home from home. Happier self-catering than in a big hotel, a motor home parked by a lake is ideal.

Places Small cruise boat. Canada; Scotland; Mauritius; Holland especially Amsterdam; Venice, Italy; Istanbul, Turkey; New York City.

Leo

You happily soak up hot sun all day. Then in the evening want to be entertained, show off your tan, and eat well. You enjoy being waited on and will pay for ostentatious service.

Places Exclusive resorts. Italy; France especially the Riviera; Prague, Czech Republic; Bombay, India; Chicago and Philadelphia.

Virgo

You like a healthy lifestyle so a cycling holiday, or organized activities suit you, preferably in clean, country air with good wholesome food served to perfection. In a city, you sightsee and improve your mind.

Places Health Farms. Switzerland; the Eastern Mediterranean; Paris and Lyon, France; Heidelburg, Germany; Boston.

Libra

Sociable and romantic, you enjoy group holidays and places you can mix with people — provided things are not too organized. You enjoy lazing around. The one thing you do not want is to be on your own.

Places Large cruise liners. Austria; Alpine regions; China; Lisbon, Portugal; Vienna, Austria; Arles, France.

Scorpio

Heat and passion are what turns Scorpio on, spiced up with a touch of danger. Underwater sports appeal. Secretive Scorpio enjoys being alone. Murder weekends bring out the detective in you — or the victim.

Places Desert islands. Tibet; Norway; North Africa particularly Fez, Morocco; Cincinnati and Washington D.C.

Sagittarius

A born traveler, Sagittarius enjoys the airport wait, but has a round-the-world ticket; or an entire railway journey planned. Destinations are not as important as traveling; you sightsee on the way.

Places Anywhere foreign. China; India; Spain; Arabia; Madagascar; Australia especially Sidney; Stuttgart, Germany; Tuscany, Italy; Toronto.

Capricorn

A hardworking sign, you do not relax easily. Climbing mountains appeals, hill walking satisfies. High ground and hard going suit you. Strongly connected with the past, you explore a bit of history along the way.

Places Mountains. India; Afghanistan; Greece; the former Yugoslavia; Brussels, Belgium; Oxford, England.

Aquarius

You like places that are different, way-out and weird. You will be first civilian on the space shuttle. Interested in humanity, and able to cope with being alone in a crowd, you enjoy foreign cities.

Places The hippy trail. Poland; Croatia; Scandinavia; Russia particularly Siberia; Los Angeles.

Pisces

Following a need to get away from it all, you head for the water and then you keep a look out for romance. How about the ultimate escapist fantasy: an island in the middle of the ocean?

Places The Oceans. Portugal; the Sahara Desert; Normandy, France; Seville, Spain; Vermont.

What's a suitable hobby for me?

Should I take an evening course? What is a good way to spend my leisure time?

While many hobbies and pastimes are carried over from childhood, there comes a time when something different is needed, maybe something more adventurous or more adult. Dowsing down a list of workshops or classes or casting the Dice is a quick way to decide. If you are stuck for ideas, astrology and your Sun sign can point out suitable hobbies for you and, who knows, these could develop into a profitable business one day.

Pendulum Dowsing

Once you have programmed your pendulum to show "yes" and "no" (see page 137), you can use it to choose a class. If you have a brochure but are not quite sure which workshop or evening class is for you, hold a pendulum with your thumb and forefinger. There should be approximately six inches of chain hanging above the page. Run your finger down the list asking "Is this the right one?" as you go down. When the pendulum swings "yes," you have your answer.

Dice

If you have yes or no questions — like whether one class or another would be better for you, ask the dice. Write your question on a piece of paper. Shake and roll two dice and let them decide.

Double Six
Definitely.

Six-Five
Probably.

Six-Four
Yes.

Six-Three
Unlikely.

Six-Two
No.

Six-One
Certainly.

Double Five
Absolutely.

Five-Four
Impossible.

Five-Three
Outside chance.

Five-Two
Maybe.

Five-One
Fifty-fifty.

Double Four
Maybe yes, maybe no.

Four-Three
Yes.

Four-Two
Unlikely.

Four-One
More likely than not.

Double Three
Yes — if you act reasonably.

Three-Two
Almost certainly.

Three-One
Almost certainly not.

Double Two
Absolutely not.

Two-One
Yes.

Double One
You cannot know.

Sun Signs

Each sign has a different emotional make-up, different qualities and different needs so it's not surprising that your Sun sign can influence leisure choices.

Aries   *Sporty and competitive.*
Field and track athletics, fencing, boxing, baseball, cycling, squash, motor racing, rock climbing, paintball, martial arts, metalwork, electronics, car maintenance, home maintenance, playing brass instruments, drama.

Taurus   *Practical and artistic.*
Yoga, dancing, wrestling, judo, football, walking, landscape gardening, singing, sculpture, cooking, eating out, collecting art or antiques, jewelry-making, carpentry and building renovation, interior decoration, painting, dressmaking, upholstery.

Gemini   *Sociable and mentally stimulated.*
T'ai chi, yoga, racquet sports, health club, playing keyboard or woodwind instruments, word games and puzzles, writing, languages, gambling, shopping, clock repairs, computers — especially the internet, the latest gadgets, investing, the movies.

Cancer   *Close to home or water.*
Sailing, fishing, swimming, wrestling, needlework, knitting, cookery, redecorating or extending the home, visiting flea markets, silver-smithing, photography, collecting antiques — especially silver, community care.

Leo *Dramatic and creative.*
Aerobics, dance, captaincy of gentle team sports, golf, amateur dramatics, theater, opera, debating, painting, jewelry-making, eating out, working for a good cause, board games.

Virgo *Practical and dextrous.*
Team games, walking, cycling, health club, yoga, crafts of all kinds, carpentry, wood carving, needlepoint, repairing electrical goods and clocks, modelmaking, studying, charity work, computers, chess.

Libra *Esthetic and artistic.*
Pair-orientated sport such as racquet games, golf, swimming, t'ai chi, dancing, health club, yoga, interior design, dressmaking and designing, garden design, reading, listening to music, painting, art exhibitions, shopping, movies, concerts, nightclubs, photography.

Scorpio *Intense and transforming.*
Martial arts, working out, jogging, diving, potholing, motor racing, reading thrillers, mysteries and magic of all kinds, metaphysics and the occult, self-improvement, barhopping, nightclubbing, computers, studying.

Sagittarius *Active and exploratory.*
Hiking, camping, snow boarding, surfing, archery, team sports, volleyball, basketball, mountain biking, horse riding, studying languages, religion, philosophy, sociology, anthropology, reading, writing, partying, traveling, animals.

Capricorn *Serious and functional.*
Hill walking, rock climbing, yoga, marathon running, structured dance, golf, genealogy and local history, gardening, home improvements, reading history and biography, community service, visiting museums, eating out, wine, pottery, art, sculpture.

Aquarius *Eclectic and far-out.*
Racquet sports, skiing, dancing, socializing, computers, UFO watching and astronomy, political or charitable work, protesting, restoring old cars or bikes, science fiction and comics, candle-making, ethnic jewelry, studying mind-body-spirit, complementary medicine.

Pisces *Artistic and fantasy-orientated.*
Fishing, swimming, sailing, dancing, solitary walking, yoga, ballet, acting, film buff, theater, photography, water color painting, metaphysics, reading, writing, poetry, romantic dinners, magic.

Western Astrology

You also can look at the pursuits suitable for the fifth house of your birthchart. If you do not know your chart, count forward five signs (see the charts on page 163). If, for example, you are a Sagittarian, your fifth house is Aries; if you are a Cancerian, it is Scorpio. Then refer to the information, above, under this sign.

Will my health remain good?

Is there something the matter with me?

Everyone is concerned about their health. People want to know whether they will enjoy good health and where potential problems may arise. While some oracles can be obscure on this point, Runes, Astrology, Palmistry, and Dowsing can be particularly helpful.

The Runes

Pulling a single rune from your rune pouch (see page 166) can alert you to potential health problems which you can then have checked out. Relevant runes are:

Laguz (Reversed) Menstrual problems, possible miscarriage. Weight gain.

Wunjo Fluid imbalances, digestive problems, menstrual difficulties.

Algiz (Reversed) Take care of your health.

Kano Heart problems.

Febu Gynecological problems.

Western Astrology

The sixth house is the house of health. If you know your birthchart, you can easily identify areas of dis-ease from the planets in this house. Saturn points to chronic or skeletal problems; Neptune is the planet of addictions and allergies. When this slippery planet is placed here, you could have taken a totally innocuous substance some years ago, only to have developed a hidden allergy that takes some years to show up. Plutonian problems are very deep and devious indeed, their causes are difficult to find and need a medical astrologer to fathom out.

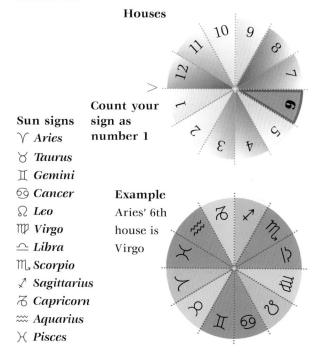

Houses

Count your sign as number 1

Sun signs
♈ Aries
♉ *Taurus*
♊ *Gemini*
♋ *Cancer*
♌ *Leo*
♍ *Virgo*
♎ *Libra*
♏ *Scorpio*
♐ *Sagittarius*
♑ *Capricorn*
♒ *Aquarius*
♓ *Pisces*

Example
Aries' 6th house is Virgo

If you don't know your birthchart, count your Sun sign as number 1 and then count counterclockwise five more signs to find the sixth house. Check the Astrological Tables on pages 185—8 to see when the planets are passing through this house.

Sun Signs

Each sign "rules" a particular part or parts of the body (see page 172). Aries, for example, is associated with the head; Cancer with the stomach, breasts, and female reproductive system; and Pisces with the feet. People with the sun in Aries tend to get headaches; with the sun in Cancer a nervous stomach, and in Pisces, foot trouble. However, there is another way of looking at the body and the zodiac to see which part of your body is most likely to trouble you.

Place a ruler on the diagram below so it passes through your birthday

(this may include part of the "arrow head") and the center to the other side. It will pass through your birth sign and the part of the body it rules. So, if you are a Taurus, it passes through your throat. But the other end shows the "shadow" part of the body linked to your sign. In Taurus' case it is Scorpio and the organs of creation and elimination. What is swallowed often affects the intestines, so you can see that Taurus also may suffer in this area. Many Taureans love their food and do tend to over-indulge and suffer accordingly.

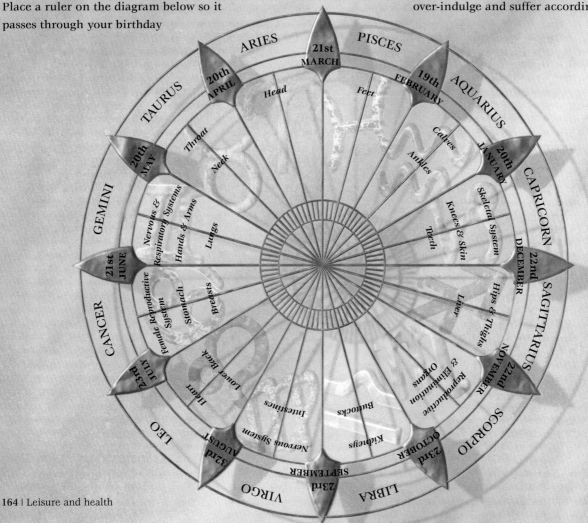

Palmistry

Palmistry can tell you a great deal about your general state of health. It is not only the palms of your hands that can indicate health — if they are sweaty, this points to thyroid problems; if they are dry, to blood pressure problems — but also your fingers and nails. Indications in the hand of health problems can be a timely warning to be checked out with a physician.

The Lines

A strong Life Line shows a constitution that shrugs off illness easily. A weaker Life Line that is chained and broken indicates a constitution that will be much more susceptible to disease. The immune system could well need building up here.

As the lines change constantly, they can be an indication of temporary disturbances but they also can indicate longstanding problems or potential difficulties. A migraine sufferer, for example, usually has a chain-like edging under the Head Line; a diabetic, a mass of small vertical lines alongside the base of the Life Line. The lines can show propensities to problems such as addiction. An alcoholic often has a characteristic thick line crossing the Life Line from under the thumb; while someone whose addiction is to drugs has a weaker line crossed by lots of small lines. Just because such signs exist, do not assume that the addiction has come into being. It could be a useful warning that would help you to avoid such problems in the future.

Fingers

A mass of fine vertical lines on your fingertips shows that you are suffering from exhaustion. Rest and recuperation is indicated. If you have deep, horizontal lines across your fingertips, you are most likely suffering from stress. If these lines are short and broken (as they often are in the hands of menopausal women), there could well be a hormonal imbalance.

Fingernails

Bluey-white nails could indicate anemia or circulation problems and yellowish ones, impaired liver function. A detox could be called for. Concave nails can indicate nutritional deficiencies, or glandular disturbances, and white spots suggest that magnesium, calcium, and vitamin C may be needed. Vertical ridges on the nails could indicate a skeletal problem; horizontal ridges usually relate to severe shock. As nails take about seven months to grow, you can date how long ago the shock occurred by how far up the nail the ridge is.

Blue-mauvey hands can indicate poor circulation or possible heart problems.

White hands could indicate anemia as well as poor circulation.

Yellow-tinged hands point to a tendency to liver problems.

Red hands point to thyroid imbalance or potential high blood pressure.

Runes

Said to have been envisioned by the Norse God Odin when he hung upside down in the World Tree, runes were traditionally made of wood but can be painted onto stones or clay tablets. They are very simple to make yourself and are usually kept in a cloth or leather bag. Runes can be read at many levels.

Making and keeping your runes

Purpose made sets of runes are available, but you can make your own. Traditionally, runes are incised onto small polished pieces of wood. Clay can also be fashioned into tablets with the sign impressed and left to dry in hot sun or a warm oven. Smooth, rounded pebbles on the beach, or flat tumbled crystals can have symbols painted with a magic marker.

Runes are traditionally kept in a draw-string bag: a rune pouch. Purchase a beautifully decorated bag or make your own out of silk or velvet.

Reversed runes

Some runes have a specific "right way up," others look the same whichever way up you place them. Reversed runes are "wrong way up."

Rune layouts

Always have a clear question in mind when you select a rune. If you want quick guidance, simply draw one rune out of the bag. For a more detailed understanding, draw three runes, one at a time. The first is the past, the situation, or the factors behind the situation; the second is the present, the action that is called for, or what you are experiencing; and the third indicates the outcome.

Mannaz *The Self*

Correct relationship to self vital. Be willing to change. Major inward growth period. Know thyself. Delay decisions. Seek advice from professional.
Reversed Look inside yourself to release blockages. Problems with authority.

Gebo *Partnership*

Time of partnership or union. Remain separate and yet be united. Implies give and take within the union. Indicates a gift, contract, or opportunity. Be prepared to pay for what you receive. (No reverse.)

Ansuz *Messenger Rune*

Focus on self change and spiritual progress. Explore the depths and receive divine love. Be receptive — look out for timely warnings. Sacred knowledge. New connections or pathways.
Reversed Failures in communication. Abuse of power, problems with authority figures.

Othila *Separation*

Radical severance. Pathways separate, old relationships end. Let go what is outworn. Inheritance or benefits.
Reversed Do not be bound by old conditioning. Go with the flow. Problems with house or goods. Possibility of theft.

Uruz *Strength*

Endings and new beginnings. Be adaptable. New birth may involve passage through darkness, do not despair. Loss may disguise an opportunity. Financial improvement.
Reversed Missed opportunity. Weakness, misplaced power, or uncontrolled strength.

Perth *Initiation*

The unknowable. Deep, secret, transformative power. Broader vision. Something hidden. Unexpected gains. Metaphysical links.
Reversed Disappointment. Do not expect too much. Look at your requirement for growth, stay in the present, do not seek outcomes. Subconscious fears.

Nauthiz *Constraint*

Severe constraint. Self preservation. Identify and work with your shadow. Expect holdups and restraints. Repay debts. Make reparation. Reconsider plans.
Reversed What is disowned brings havoc. Tension. A dark passage. Inability to let go. Control anger.

Inguz *Fertility*

A new pathway. Intuition. Completion is essential — prioritize. Need to share. Strength to find resolution or clarification. Remain centered. Emergence of the new. Freedom from a rut or old patterns. (No reverse.)

Runes *(continued)*

Eithwaz *Defense* A time of waiting. Have patience, blockages may be beneficial and growth promoted. Make clear decisions but do not strive. Adapt to situations, take a step backward or aside if necessary. Find another way around the problem. (No reverse.)

Algiz *Protection* Right action and conduct are important. Control your emotions. Do not avoid pain, go with it. Opportunities await. Be creative.
Reversed Be careful with your health. Beware people who use you or act illegally. Be responsible.

Febu *Possessions* A promise of nourishment and fulfillment. Reassess your attitude to wealth and possessions, is it for your growth? Conserve what you have. Share your good fortune.
Reversed Frustration and losses. Doubtful situations. Recognize where true nourishment lies.

Wunjo *Joy* The end of struggle, you have found yourself. New clarity, joy, and happiness. Emotional balance. Spiritual or artistic awakening. New energy emerges.
Reversed Avoid major decisions, judgment is poor. Possible female health problems.

Jera *Harvest* End of a cycle. Turn of the season. Inevitable change. Fresh start or house move. Beneficial outcome may take one year. Patiently reap what has been sown. Be alert to opportunities that could be missed, do not resist change. (No reverse.)

Kano *Opening* Illumination, mental clarity. Creativity. The start of work or relationship. Celebration. Health and healing.
Reversed Darkness descends. Endings, losses, give them up gladly and wait to be re-illuminated. Possible heart problems, low immunity.

Teiwaz *Warrior* Courage, passion, aggression. Powerful new relationship: lust, anger, angst. Ability to cut away what is outworn. Venture into your depths.
Reversed Broken love affair, sexual frustration or obsession. Accidents. Energy leakage. Are you dominating another?

Berkana *Growth* Fertility and new beginnings. Awakening of the life force. Weddings and births. Dispersing resistance. New developments. Joy within the family.
Reversed Plans do not reach fruition. Life fails to grow, identify blocks. Be diligent. Energy lacking.

Ehwaz *Movement* Time of transition. Something new. Travel, movement, transport. Steady progress and transformation — business or relationships. Face the future with confidence.
Reversed Immobility. Movement blocked. Problems with transport. Is what you are doing timely?

Laguz *Flow*

Fluidity, receptivity, birth. Intuitive knowing. Protection and safety. Time to go with the flow. Emotional and comfort needs satisfied. Cleansing or re-evaluation needed. Sacred marriage.

Reversed Do not overreach yourself. Failure to use intuition. Female health problems. Addiction.

Hagalaz *Elemental Power*

Sudden change, chaos, freedom. "Bolt from blue." Natural disaster. Family problems. Breaking free of restrictions. Events beyond your control. Be forewarned of disasters. More severe the disruption, more significant the outcome. (No reverse.)

Raido *Communication*

Communication on all levels. Movement. Changes in affairs. The soul's journey. Self healing. Union with the divine. Cut away illusions.

Reversed Breaks in personal relationships. Difficulty in travel. Lack of imagination. Opportunities re-routed.

Thurisaz *Gateway*

Inner and outer work. Non action: allow matters to run their course. Contact the divine through contemplation and self-examination. Let go past. Protection.

Reversed Avoid hasty decisions. Integrate new growth. Misplaced power, over-sensitivity.

Dagaz *Breakthrough*

Transformation. Major shift or breakthrough. Transformed attitudes. Clarity and recognition. Success in examinations. Have trust: outcome is assured, though unpredictable. May indicate period of prosperity or achievement (depending on other runes). (No reverse.)

Isa *Standstill*

Difficult period. Impediments, obstacles, powerlessness. Feelings, plans, frozen. Sacrifice of long-held desire. Let go old habits, release past. Sacrifice of the ego. Remain isolated, you cannot rely on support of others. Trust your process. Have patience, the thaw will come. (No reverse.)

Sowelu *Wholeness*

Self-realization. Express your essence creatively. Bring your talents into the light. Guard your energy: time for recharging and regeneration, healing and recuperation. Take a holiday. Let light flow into your shadows. Do without doing. (No reverse.)

The Blank Rune *The Unknowable*

Everything is possible. Relinquish control. Be willing, do not try to force what has not yet formed. Contact with your destiny. Karmic reckoning and release. Deepest fears surface — let go. Symbolic death of the old. The new unfolds. (No reverse.)

What remedy should I try?

Will I recover soon?

Is now a good time to diet?

There are a number of oracles that can help you choose a possible remedy for illness or ill health and also can indicate the probable length of any illness. Dowsing, either with your body or a pendulum can give a quick "yes or no" answer to a wide range of questions dealing with health and can help you pick an efficacious remedy. Looking at your birthchart will give you lots of health advice, here specifically about whether to diet or not. Geomancy can answer whether recovery will be soon and also identify underlying problems.

Body Dowsing

Your body can be used for dowsing. Have a question in mind such as "Will reflexology be good for me?" then simply make a loop with the first finger and thumb of one hand and loop the finger and thumb of the other hand through. Close tight and pull. If your thumb and finger hold, the answer is "yes." If they part, the answer is "no." You can use this to answer all kinds of yes/no questions but it is particularly useful when looking at appropriate foods (will it say "yes" to that chocolate cake?) and appropriate therapies.

Pendulum Dowsing

As dowsing is connected to body awareness, you can dowse for remedies to make you feel better physically or emotionally, for therapies that will work for you, and to answer simple yes/no questions like "Should I have plastic surgery?" To do this you will need to have established your "yes" and "no" swing (see page 137).

If you are drawn to the subtle, energy-based Bach Flower Remedies, for instance, you can spread the chart out on a table, holding the corners down, if necessary. Working in a clockwise direction, put one finger on each remedy in turn. Hold the pendulum in your other hand and ask "Is this the right remedy for me at this time?" If the answer is "no" move onto the next. If the answer is "yes," it is still wise to check out the rest of the chart as you may need more than one remedy.

Geomancy

Random marks on paper can be used to create a prophetic figure. Make four lines of random dashes across a piece of paper one below the other (do not count as you go). Add up the number of dashes in each line. At the end of each odd-numbered line, put a large dot •. At the end of each even-numbered line, put two large dots ••. If your figure looks like one of the following, the message is clear.

 Laetitia Good health and recovery from illness.

 Fortuna major Look within to find the answers.

 Rubeus Strong emotions creating problems.

If your figure is not one of the above, refer to page 81 where you will find the meanings of the other figures. You also can construct a geomantic chart to see whether you will get better soon. The chart could well help you to identify factors holding back your recovery. The sixth house of the chart is where you find your illnesses, the first house is where your vitality lies.

Is This a Good Time to Diet?

The Zodiac signs are said to "rule" different parts of the body and the planets, too, have their physiological correspondences. But it is the movement of the planets overhead in the sky that can help you to answer questions like the above. Jupiter, one of the biggest planets, is the planet of expansion. When Jupiter hovers around the Sun in your birthchart, you somehow just can't help putting on weight! So starting a diet for your birthday has little chance of success. You need to have begun well before that.

The Ascendant in your chart represents the face you present to the world. When Jupiter moves over the Ascendant you tend to expand in all directions, physically as well as mentally and emotionally. Here again, a diet is going to be hard work. When Jupiter moves on in the cycle, however, and is opposite to either your Sun or Ascendant, weight begins to fall off. Dieting is then easy.

As Jupiter takes a year to move around your chart, you will have two opportunities a year to lose weight quickly. Check with the Astrological Tables (see pages 185–8) for your optimum moments — when Jupiter is in your sixth house. If you don't know your birthchart, put the Sun at the start of house one. Count off six signs to find the one that is your sixth house (see diagrams page 163).

How can I cope with stress?

Many illnesses are actually a state of dis-ease — the body is not at ease with itself. Usually there is a stress or imbalance at the bottom of the problem. The Sun signs react to stress in different ways — some thrive on it, others cannot tolerate it at all. Tissue salts are very gentle remedies that help you cope with stress and imbalances that can occur in the body. Each Sun sign resonates to a specific tissue salt. Taking one, available from any health store, could well transform your life.

Sun signs and parts of the body

Each sign is said to "rule" a certain part of the body:

Aries *Head*

Taurus *Throat and neck*

Gemini *Nervous system, hands and arms, lungs and respiratory system*

Cancer *Stomach, breasts, female reproductive system*

Leo *Heart and lower back (lumbar region)*

Virgo *Nervous system, intestines*

Libra *Kidneys and buttocks*

Scorpio *Reproductive and elimination organs*

Sagittarius *Hips, thighs, and liver*

Capricorn *Skeletal system, knees, skin, and teeth*

Aquarius *Calves and ankles*

Pisces *Feet*

Aries
Usually thrives on stress but too much tension leads to headaches. Strong constitution. Prone to fevers, digestive problems, migraines.
For optimum health Eat regular, balanced meals, rest, and exercise.
Tissue salt *Kali. Phos. (Potassium Phosphate)*

Taurus
Dislikes and suppresses stress, which goes to throat. Strong constitution. Prone to weight problems, metabolic imbalances, laryngitis, and stiff neck.
For optimum health Let off steam through exercise, massage; watch what you eat.
Tissue salt *Nat. Sulph. (Sodium Sulphate)*

Gemini
Thrives on stress. Resilient. Prone to nervous conditions, coughs, sprains or broken bones.
For optimum health Relax and get enough sleep; take regular exercise; supplement good meals with vitamins.
Tissue salt *Kali. Mur. (Potassium Chloride)*

Cancer
Dislikes stress which goes to stomach. Recovers quickly. Immune system is strongly affected by emotions. Prone to digestive problems.
For optimum health Keep your emotions balanced, give up worrying, let go resentment, eat regularly.
Tissue salt *Calc. Fluor. (Calcium Fluoride)*

Leo
Usually dislikes stress, which affects back or heart. Strong constitution. Prone to high blood pressure, heart disease, lower back pain.
For optimum health Exercise regularly; avoid over-indulgence, stress, and anger.
Tissue salt *Mag. Phos. (Magnesium Phosphate)*

Virgo
May run on nervous energy, but stress takes toll on guts. Slightly delicate constitution. Prone to psychosomatic problems, hypochondria, irritable bowel syndrome, eczema.
For optimum health Relax, stop worrying, don't be too self-critical.
Tissue salt *Kali. Sulph. (Potassium Sulphate)*

Libra
Laid-back. Sensitive constitution. When stressed toxic conditions result in headaches, chronic fatigue. Metabolism may be sluggish.
For optimum health Avoid late nights and over-rich food, detox regularly, pamper yourself.
Tissue salt *Nat. Phos. (Sodium Phosphate)*

Scorpio
Uses stress but too much can cause drop off in libido. Resilient constitution. Prone to nervous tension in shoulders and neck. May become toxic.
For optimum health Let go, stop pushing yourself, talk things over, detox.
Tissue salt *Calc. Sulph. (Calcium Sulphate)*

Sagittarius
Goes flat out then eventually crashes. Stress usually affects Gemini parts such as lungs. Recovers quickly. Prone to liver problems, arthritis, rheumatism in hips.
For optimum health Exercise body and mind; avoid over-indulgence.
Tissue salt *Silica (Silica Oxide)*

Capricorn
Thrives on pressure. Not knowing when to stop weakens immune system. Skin or skeleton react but stress may hit Cancerian stomach. Prone to joint problems, tooth decay, depression, chronic fatigue.
For optimum health Learn when to let go; walk, relax, look after your teeth.
Tissue salt *Calc. Phos. (Calcium Phosphate)*

Aquarius
Often thrives on stress and does not relax until total collapse occurs. Stress usually affects Leonine opposites, heart or back. Prone to circulatory problems, sprained ankles, sudden ills that vanish quickly.
For optimum health Slow down, exercise, play, have back massage, use complementary medicine.
Tissue salt *Nat. Mur. (Sodium Chloride)*

Pisces
Adapts to stress by flowing this way and that, but eventually succumbs. Sensitive constitution, exacerbated by emotions. Prone to addictions, psychosomatic ills, bunions.
For optimum health Watch your emotions, relax, avoid drink and drugs, look after your feet, use reflexology.
Tissue salt *Ferr. Phos. (Iron Phosphate)*

Will I live long?

Many people ask when they will die. Reputable fortune tellers and wise oracles never answer this question because death is not a finite thing. Palmistry, however, provides a clue, but even this needs clarification.

Palmistry

Your Life Line is said to indicate your health and the length of your life. However, as can be seen from the two hand prints here, lines can vary considerably from the left hand to the right. The left hand Life Line is very short and ends abruptly near to the Fate Line at around age 25. It could be said to indicate an early death. The Life Line on the right hand is much longer, indicating living to a ripe old age. So how can two lines conflict so badly? Well, this person had a near-death experience at age 25 that resulted in a totally new life — which started just before her thirtieth birthday (when the Fate Line ends). It is as though she stepped totally outside her fate and became a new person. That person looks set to live well into old age.

   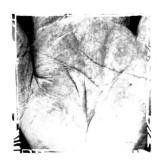

Right Palm   **Left Palm**

Death

An oracle might indicate death, but this would not necessarily be physical death. It could be the end of a cycle, or a total and drastic change in life so powerful that it appears the old you has died and a new you is emerging — which would be better described as a rebirth. It could be something passing out of your life — a job, a person or a place. If oracles are interpreted too literally, you could live in fear and dread either your own death or that of a loved one, only to find that this was not what the oracle meant. On the other hand, a physical death could be indicated, but only a few people would have the wisdom to handle this well — "putting their house in order" and saying their goodbyes, for instance. Other people would have it hanging over them like a black cloud and not enjoy their last days, so it would be non-productive for this to be stated categorically. If death has to be mentioned at all, it is much kinder for this to be expressed as a possibility that has not yet come into manifestation, and which might not do so in the foreseeable future. This enables preparations to be made, but does not paralyze the future.

Life Cycles

and

Charts

Life Cycles

From careful observation, ancient peoples postulated a series of unfolding cycles operating throughout human life. Some are cosmological and astrological "Great Ages" spreading over eons of time, or shorter periods encompassing the orbits of planets such as Saturn or Jupiter. Other cycles are more personal, based on an individual's date of birth as in Numerology, Nine Star Ki and Cosmic Rhythms.

Knowledge of these cycles was gathered together into a body of occult or hidden knowledge that was passed down the millennia. One such cycle is a progressive seven-year unfoldment moving from birth to death. It is this cycle on which Shakespeare, a writer whose work contains much esoteric knowledge, drew for his Seven Ages of Man. While his description relates to Seven Ages rather than seven year cycles, it nevertheless fits in with the shorter life expectancy of his day as seven times seven would be the average age of death in Elizabethan England. His Seven Ages encompass the major physical and emotional developmental stages mapped out in the seven year cycles. Shakespeare's Seven Ages also relate to the rulership over life stages by the seven astrological planets known in his day. Planets that impart individual specific attributes such as nurturing and the emotions (the Moon), the mind and communication (Mercury), love and values (Venus), will and aggression (Mars), and the religious impulse and ethics (Jupiter) in the development of the self (the Sun). It is not only the experience of an Elizabethan man that Shakespeare's graphic description mirrors, modern man (or woman) equally can relate to his picture of unfolding fate.

Midlife Crisis

The astrological midlife crisis occurs when Uranus is opposite its place in your natal chart. As Uranus is an unpredictable planet that moves erratically, this can happen anytime between 39 and 46, but the most usual age is around 42–44. This is a time of upheaval and change, when the unlived life demands attention and you question your purpose and direction. It often coincides with redundancy or health problems that force a change of perspective or affect your working life. Even though it may feel like a disaster, it is an opportunity that allows new parts of yourself to come into prominence. A change of career is a common feature of midlife crisis.

Cosmic rhythms

Better known as biorhythms, these are innate, personal inner rhythms arising from the moment of birth. If you understand cosmic rhythms you can attune to your own natural cycle of activity — periods of rest and recuperation or moments of creativity and natural expansiveness — and use it to manifest a better future.

The Personal Life Cycle

Based on an ancient cycle of seven year periods progressively unfolding throughout life, each period in The Personal Life Cycle concentrates on certain areas that must be successfully developed in order for the whole person to evolve. The development goes from discovering oneself as an individual at the physical, emotional, and mental levels to the development of spiritual awareness and unity with the whole.

0 to 7 *The First Seven Year Period*
Self-discovery. Control of the body, communication, and relationship to the environment. Cultural identity established.

7 to 14 *The Second Seven Year Period*
Personal and gender identity established. Physical characteristics mature, mental abilities unfold.

14 to 21 *The Third Seven Year Period*
Physiology and personality matures. Sense of responsibility develops, capabilities become apparent.

21 to 28 *The Fourth Seven Year Period*
Emotional development. Unfolding of intuition and interest in the arts.

28 to 35 *The Fifth Seven Year Period*
Creativity and mental development. Success in business. Attunement begins to cosmic consciousness.

35 to 42 *The Sixth Seven Year Period*
Moving beyond personal attainment. Development of humanitarian aims. Sharing resources with others.

42 to 49 *The Seventh Seven Year Period*
Emergence of a new person with new goals and ideals. Thoughts turn to spirituality and working for the community.

49 to 56 *The Eighth Seven Year Period*
Moving still further away from personal ambition and into a spiritual being. Physical vitality declines but mental and psychic prowess increase to compensate.

56 to 63 *The Ninth Seven Year Period*
Mental and physical faculties slow down as the spiritual emerges more strongly.

The Remaining Seven Year Periods
Emphasis is placed more strongly on the recognition that you are a spiritual being.

The Individual Yearly Cycle

Based on seven periods of approximately 52 days, The Individual Yearly Cycle runs over a year — but not a calendar one. It runs from birthday to birthday. This gives you your own unique yearly cycle. A cycle which is calculated by counting forward from your birthday. The Individual Yearly Cycle can show you when to set things in motion, when to rest and enjoy yourself, when to travel or when to speculate. The Health Cycle also follows the same fifty-two day cycles.

Method
Write your birthday on a piece of paper. Using the perpetual calendar (see overleaf), count forward 52 days and write down that day and month. The space between the two is the first period. Count forward another 52 days, writing down the beginning and end of the period, until you have seven periods in all. You may find that the last period does not work out exactly to the day before your birthday. If so, simply write down the day before your birthday as the last day. (For an at-a-glance record of the cycles, photocopy the calendar and mark the 52 day periods with different highlighter pens.)

Period 1 *(the first 52 days)*
This is the period during which you can beneficially ask favors or seek employment, advancement, reward, or recognition — especially from those in power. The cosmic vibrations favor moving forward at this time.
Health cycle Constitution strong, vitality at its best. Take exercise, eat wisely, and avoid foods that overheat. Good for operations or health regimes.

Period 2 *(the second 52 days)*
This period favors journeys, especially those of short duration, and moving house or changing your job. It supports short-term changes and those that occur quickly. It is not conducive to new business plans or

investment, or finding a new career. Nor should you sign long-term contracts now, or speculate or borrow money. If you buy a house during this period, you will not stay there long.

Health cycle Short-term physical and emotional disturbances. Attend to them quickly and do not allow the mind to brood on them.

Period 3 *(the third 52 days)*

The impulse to act is strong and vitality high. Directed carefully, this urge can bring about great things in business or in activities that call for high physical energy. It can overcome competitors, and obstacles that have held you back, although you should be wary of signing contracts and agreements. It is good for salespeople or teachers who use fiery oratory to convince. The kind of mastery called for is persistent and hard-working. Carelessly used, there is a danger of misjudgment. Women may find this period helpful, especially those seeking the aid of men, but it also can lead to arguments.

Health cycle More prone to accidents, injury, or operations. Keep warm; tendency toward cold. Avoid over-work and over-eating. Watch blood pressure and cleanse the blood.

Period 4 *(the fourth 52 day period)*

During this optimistic period it is the mental and intuitive processes that are favored. Creativity and self-expression are enhanced. An excellent time to study. Thoughts are quick and to the point. New ideas abound. Act quickly to make the most of these and bring them into practical expression. However, deception could be practiced, so check your sources and watch out for fraud. This is not a good time to marry, to buy a house, or accept a business proposition.

Health cycle Tendency to nervous strain. Avoid too much study. Sleep and rest whenever possible.

Period 5 *(the fifth 52 day period)*

The success period for personal matters. They expand, grow, and come to fruition. Prosperity increases. You feel sociable, beneficent, and drawn toward higher

Perpetual Calendar

Jan	1 2 3 4 5 6 7 8 9 10 11 12 13 14 15 16 17 18 19 20 21 22 23 24 25 26 27 28 29 30 31
Feb	1 2 3 4 5 6 7 8 9 10 11 12 13 14 15 16 17 18 19 20 21 22 23 24 25 26 27 28[29]
Mar	1 2 3 4 5 6 7 8 9 10 11 12 13 14 15 16 17 18 19 20 21 22 23 24 25 26 27 28 29 30 31
Apr	1 2 3 4 5 6 7 8 9 10 11 12 13 14 15 16 17 18 19 20 21 22 23 24 25 26 27 28 29 30
May	1 2 3 4 5 6 7 8 9 10 11 12 13 14 15 16 17 18 19 20 21 22 23 24 25 26 27 28 29 30 31
Jun	1 2 3 4 5 6 7 8 9 10 11 12 13 14 15 16 17 18 19 20 21 22 23 24 25 26 27 28 29 30
Jul	1 2 3 4 5 6 7 8 9 10 11 12 13 14 15 16 17 18 19 20 21 22 23 24 25 26 27 28 29 30 31
Aug	1 2 3 4 5 6 7 8 9 10 11 12 13 14 15 16 17 18 19 20 21 22 23 24 25 26 27 28 29 30 31
Sep	1 2 3 4 5 6 7 8 9 10 11 12 13 14 15 16 17 18 19 20 21 22 23 24 25 26 27 28 29 30
Oct	1 2 3 4 5 6 7 8 9 10 11 12 13 14 15 16 17 18 19 20 21 22 23 24 25 26 27 28 29 30 31
Nov	1 2 3 4 5 6 7 8 9 10 11 12 13 14 15 16 17 18 19 20 21 22 23 24 25 26 27 28 29 30
Dec	1 2 3 4 5 6 7 8 9 10 11 12 13 14 15 16 17 18 19 20 21 22 23 24 25 26 27 28 29 30 31

ideals. Philosophy or metaphysics appeal. An excellent time to begin long journeys or undertakings that require favorable influences to bring them to completion. You can collect money that is owed to you, speculate, or borrow — as long as such matters are legitimate.

Health cycle Health should be good, especially with exercise and fresh air. Excellent for recovering from fevers or chronic illness. Practice positive thinking. Avoid over-indulgence.

Period 6 *(the sixth 52 day period)*

This is the time to seek amusement, culture and relaxation. It is beneficial for short journeys that are specifically for pleasure, but avoid long journeys and those on water. An excellent time for business — especially those concerned with the arts. Speculation, friendship, and the ordinary affairs of life are favored.

Health cycle Over-indulgence or mental strain could affect skin, throat, and kidneys. Drink plenty of water, exercise outdoors.

Period 7 *(the seventh 52 day period)*

A critical and disruptive time. Depression and despondency are common. Things break down in order that something new may emerge. Other things hang fire or end disruptively. A business that has been going badly could go bankrupt now if care is not exercised. Impulsive behavior could cause disaster. Postpone pending matters until after your birthday (act in the first or second period for success). A good period for dealing with the elderly or with real estate. A most unfavorable period for starting a new business or for journeys of any kind.

Health cycle Chronic conditions may set in. Stay away from public places to avoid colds and fevers as immune system weak. Tendency to depression and despondency. Avoid operations or new health regime.

The Business Cycle

In exactly the same way that people have an unfolding cycle, businesses, plans, or associations also have a distinct cycle of their own. Attuning to these cycles makes it easier to expand the business, to retrench, or even to choose an appropriate moment to retire.

The business cycle can be used for an actual business or profession, or it can be used to look at something altruistic like a charity or organization. It can profitably be used to monitor the progress of plans and intentions you may have.

The birthday of a business is usually taken as the first day it begins trading or the start of its financial year. However, you can use the day when the idea for the business was first mooted.

Method

When you have ascertained the birthday of the business — which could be when you first had the idea, or the grand opening, the start of a bank account, the renting of premises, and the like — use the perpetual calendar (see page 178) to calculate the fifty-two day periods as for the personal cycles.

Business Period One

This is the time to promote the business, to bring it to the attention of the public and to capitalize on good will. It is not the most auspicious cycle for sales; you are laying the groundwork and will see the rewards shortly. Plan and execute a corporate advertising or publicity campaign, attend conferences or give interviews. If you need endorsements for your products or services, or political backing, seek them now. Excellent for dealing with officials of any kind.

Business Period Two

Try out short-term plans and make important, if temporary, changes in key personnel. Unfavorable for

Life Cycles (continued)

new contracts and agreements unless these are legally watertight. Verbal arrangements could fail. Contact clients or customers to capitalize on established business relationships.

Business Period Three

During this highly energized cycle, promote the business. Construct, expand, go all out for production and sales but watch out for saboteurs, accidents, and explosions. Problems with competitors possible. Set up accounting systems and press for payment of bills by letter but not in court. Other legal matters are favored and can be pursued vigorously.

Business Period Four

Another excellent period for self-promotion and advertising, especially mailings. Also good for new contracts and agreements, provided you guard against deception.

Business Period Five

Financial growth period. The best period for sales and distribution. A rapid return can be expected. An ideal time to invest, extend, and seek credit. Advantageous for debt collecting, including court action. Ideal time to promote the business abroad.

Business Period Six

Time for rest and relaxation where possible. Send key executives on vacation. A good time for anything connected with the arts, luxury items, and culture. Excellent for meeting the public or valued customers and for establishing partnerships or subsidiaries. Buy stocks and shares now.

Business Period Seven

A conservative time of consolidation and planning restructuring where needed. Do not put new plans or alliances into action until this period ends. Avoid radical change but put in hand necessary change where it relates to letting go the past so that reconstruction can begin when the cycle is over. Consult with retired persons if advice needed.

The Charts

On the following pages, you will find a variety of charts that you may need to consult to find out what the oracle has to tell you.

Chinese Animal Years

The Chinese calendar is based on a lunar cycle and its start changes from year to year. Each year also is given the name of one of twelve animals. If you are not sure which animal year is that of your birth, look down the left-hand dates of each animal until you find your year. For example, if you were born in 1974, you will find it under the year of the Tiger. Check to see that your birthday is included in the dates shown. If your birthday is prior to the date written (for example, you were born on January 18th), then refer to the animal above (find the year on the right-hand side). You will be an Ox.

Nine Star Ki Numbers

In the Western calendar, the year starts on January 1, but in Nine Star Ki, it usually begins on February 3rd, 4th, or 5th. The chart shown on page 183, gives the start of the years from 1910 to 2017, including the exact date and time (Greenwich Mean Time or GMT) each year begins. Use it to look up your Nine Star Ki number.

Start by locating your birth year, which is shown at the top of each individual box. If you were born in 1965 on or after the 7:57 a.m. GMT on February 4th, you'd be a number 8. If you were born anytime between January 1 and before 7:57 a.m. on February 4, you are a 9 — the number for 1964.

If you were born close to February 3rd, 4th, or 5th in any year, you will need to take account of the difference between the GMT on the chart and your local time. New York is five hours behind GMT, for example, so the year changes in New York five hours earlier than in GMT — the time shown on the chart. In 1979 the year began on February 4th at 17:21 GMT, so in New York it would have begun at 17:21 minus 5 hours or 12:21 p.m. local time. The same applies when calculating dates for moving or finding favorable directions using the chart on page 184. If you plan to move home on February 4, 2003 before 13:08 GMT, refer to the chart for 2002. In New York the equivalent time for February 4, 2003 would be before 8:08 a.m. If you are determining a favorable move, the directions for 2002 would be the most auspicious ones.

Favorable Directions

In Nine Star Ki, each direction has a certain type of ki energy and this can influence your own personal ki energy in a positive or negative way. A favorable direction can help you achieve your goals. It is important, therefore, that you choose a direction carefully when moving house, when looking for a job, or when traveling. To determine which directions will contribute to a favorable move for you, refer to the chart on page 184. Having determined your Nine Ki number (see above) look for the box on the right side of the chart that corresponds. Your number also is associated with a color. The most auspicious directions for you each year are indicated wherever you see the color associated with your Nine Star Ki number. For example, if you are a number 2, in 2003 East-Northeast and West are two favorable directions while in 2004, there are three favorable directions — South, West, and Northwest.

Astrological Tables

The movements of the planets around the sky, charted by actual observation, follow a regular pattern. Once every year, the Earth makes a complete journey around the Sun, and the Sun is said to enter and leave each sign at specific times. This has given rise to Sun sign astrology, which is an easy system to follow but not completely accurate as the Sun's entry into each sign varies somewhat from year to year.

It is, however, possible to know not only when the Sun exactly enters a particular sign but also when all the planets enter a particular sign. This is done through ephemerides, the tabulated movements of the planets. On pages 185–8, you will find an abbreviated version of planetary movements, showing the approximate position of Jupiter, Mercury, Venus, Mars, and Saturn during the period 2000–2012. For exact placements, you would have to consult an astrological ephemeris or astrologer.

At the top of each page you will find a guide to the signs. The signs appear on the left-hand columns and next to them the dates — day, month, year when the planet enters each sign. If, for example, you want to attract love and romance into your life, you'll want to know when your Venus is going to visit your Fifth (Love Affairs) house. If you are a Taurean, your Fifth house is Virgo. Look at the chart on page 187 and locate the sign for Virgo on the left-hand column. Now look alongside, and you will notice that Venus is in Virgo from August 6 to August 30, 2000; from September 20 to October 10, 2001; from July 10 to August 7, 2002; from August 22 to September 15, 2003; and so on.

Chinese Animal Years

Year of the Horse
1930 Jan 30 to Feb 16 1931
1942 Feb 15 to Feb 4 1943
1954 Feb 3 to Jan 23 1955
1966 Jan 21 to Feb 8 1967
1978 Feb 7 to Jan 27 1979
1990 Jan 27 to Feb 14 1991
2002 Feb 12 to Jan 31 2003

Year of the Rooster
1933 Jan 26 to Feb 13 1934
1945 Feb 13 to Feb 1 1946
1957 Jan 31 to Feb 17 1958
1969 Feb 17 to Feb 5 1970
1981 Feb 5 to Jan 24 1982
1993 Jan 23 to Feb 9 1994
2005 Feb 9 to Jan 28 2006

Year of the Rat
1936 Jan 24 to Feb 10 1937
1948 Feb 10 to Jan 28 1949
1960 Jan 28 to Feb 14 1961
1972 Feb 15 to Feb 2 1973
1984 Feb 2 to Feb 19 1985
1996 Feb 19 to Feb 6 1997
2008 Feb 7 to Jan 25 2009

Year of the Rabbit
1939 Feb 19 to Feb 7 1940
1951 Feb 6 to Jan 26 1952
1963 Jan 25 to Feb 12 1964
1975 Feb 11 to Jan 30 1976
1987 Jan 29 to Feb 16 1988
1999 Feb 16 to Feb 4 2000
2011 Feb 3 to Jan 22 2012

Year of the Ram
1931 Feb 17 to Feb 5 1932
1943 Feb 5 to Jan 24 1944
1955 Jan 24 to Feb 11 1956
1967 Feb 9 to Jan 29 1968
1979 Jan 28 to Feb 15 1980
1991 Feb 15 to Feb 3 1992
2003 Feb 1 to Jan 21 2004

Year of the Dog
1934 Feb 14 to Feb 3 1935
1946 Feb 2 to Jan 21 1947
1958 Feb 18 to Feb 7 1959
1970 Feb 6 to Jan 26 1971
1982 Jan 25 to Feb 12 1983
1994 Feb 10 to Jan 30 1995
2006 Jan 29 to Feb 27 2007

Year of the Ox
1937 Feb 11 to Jan 30 1938
1949 Jan 29 to Feb 16 1950
1961 Feb 15 to Feb 4 1962
1973 Feb 3 to Jan 22 1974
1985 Feb 20 to Feb 8 1986
1997 Feb 7 to Jan 27 1998
2009 Jan 26 to Feb 13 2010

Year of the Dragon
1940 Feb 8 to Jan 26 1941
1952 Jan 27 to Feb 13 1953
1964 Feb 13 to Feb 1 1965
1976 Jan 31 to Feb 17 1977
1988 Feb 17 to Feb 5 1989
2000 Feb 5 to Jan 23 2001
2012 Jan 23 to Feb 9 2013

Year of the Monkey
1932 Feb 6 to Jan 25 1933
1944 Jan 25 to Feb 12 1945
1956 Feb 12 to Jan 30 1957
1968 Jan 30 to Feb 16 1969
1980 Feb 16 to Feb 4 1981
1992 Feb 4 to Jan 22 1993
2004 Jan 22 to Feb 8 2005

Year of the Pig
1935 Feb 4 to Jan 23 1936
1947 Jan 22 to Feb 9 1948
1959 Feb 8 to Jan 27 1960
1971 Jan 27 to Feb 14 1972
1983 Feb 13 to Feb 1 1984
1995 Jan 31 to Feb 18 1996
2007 Feb 18 to Feb 6 2008

Year of the Tiger
1938 Jan 31 to Feb 18 1939
1950 Feb 17 to Feb 5 1951
1962 Feb 5 to Jan 24 1963
1974 Jan 23 to Feb 10 1975
1986 Feb 9 to Jan 28 1987
1998 Jan 28 to Feb 15 1999
2010 Feb 14 to Feb 2 2011

Year of the Snake
1941 Jan 27 to Feb 14 1942
1953 Feb 14 to Feb 2 1954
1965 Feb 2 to Jan 20 1966
1977 Feb 18 to Feb 6 1978
1989 Feb 6 to Jan 25 1990
2001 Jan 24 to Feb 11 2002
2013 Feb 10 to Jan 30 2014

Nine Star Ki Numbers

Your year number	9	8	7	6	5	4	3	2	1
Year Beginning date Time (GMT)	1910 4 Feb 23:41	1911 5 Feb 05:33	1912 5 Feb 11:11	1913 4 Feb 17:01	1914 4 Feb 22:53	1915 5 Feb 04:34	1916 5 Feb 10:31	1917 4 Feb 16:18	1918 4 Feb 22:06
	1919 5 Feb 04:00	1920 5 Feb 09:43	1921 5 Feb 15:34	1922 4 Feb 21:28	1923 5 Feb 03:13	1924 5 Feb 09:06	1925 4 Feb 14:58	1926 4 Feb 20:49	1927 5 Feb 02:46
	1928 5 Feb 08:31	1929 4 Feb 14:19	1930 4 Feb 20:11	1931 5 Feb 01:53	1932 5 Feb 07:42	1933 4 Feb 13:28	1934 4 Feb 19:13	1935 5 Feb 01:03	1936 5 Feb 06:47
	1937 4 Feb 12:36	1938 4 Feb 18:32	1939 5 Feb 00:20	1940 5 Feb 06:15	1941 4 Feb 12:07	1942 4 Feb 17:57	1943 4 Feb 23:51	1944 5 Feb 05:39	1945 5 Feb 11:26
	1946 4 Feb 17:18	1947 4 Feb 23:03	1948 5 Feb 04:50	1949 4 Feb 10:40	1950 4 Feb 16:29	1951 4 Feb 22:29	1952 5 Feb 04:07	1953 4 Feb 09:52	1954 4 Feb 15:42
	1955 4 Feb 21:29	1956 5 Feb 03:15	1957 4 Feb 09:07	1958 4 Feb 14:57	1959 4 Feb 20:47	1960 5 Feb 02:38	1961 4 Feb 08:29	1962 4 Feb 14:24	1963 4 Feb 20:17
	1964 5 Feb 02:08	1965 4 Feb 07:57	1966 4 Feb 13:46	1967 4 Feb 19:32	1968 5 Feb 01:19	1969 4 Feb 07:04	1970 4 Feb 12:50	1971 4 Feb 18:37	1972 5 Feb 00:23
	1973 4 Feb 06:13	1974 4 Feb 12:08	1975 4 Feb 17:56	1976 4 Feb 23:48	1977 4 Feb 05:38	1978 4 Feb 11:28	1979 4 Feb 17:21	1980 4 Feb 23:10	1981 4 Feb 04:59
	1982 4 Feb 10:53	1983 4 Feb 16:38	1984 4 Feb 22:27	1985 4 Feb 04:18	1986 4 Feb 10:05	1987 4 Feb 15:57	1988 4 Feb 21:42	1989 4 Feb 05:28	1990 4 Feb 09:20
	1991 4 Feb 15:04	1992 4 Feb 20:51	1993 4 Feb 02:42	1994 4 Feb 08:27	1995 4 Feb 14:18	1996 4 Feb 20:10	1997 4 Feb 02:00	1998 4 Feb 08:01	1999 4 Feb 13:51
	2000 4 Feb 19:39	2001 4 Feb 01:35	2002 4 Feb 07:20	2003 4 Feb 13:08	2004 4 Feb 18:57	2005 4 Feb 00:38	2006 4 Feb 06:31	2007 4 Feb 12:16	2008 4 Feb 17:59
	2009 3 Feb 23:55	2010 4 Feb 05:40	2011 4 Feb 11:31	2012 4 Feb 17:28	2013 3 Feb 23:05	2014 4 Feb 05:05	2015 4 Feb 10:55	2016 4 Feb 16:40	2017 3 Feb 22:37

Favorable Directions

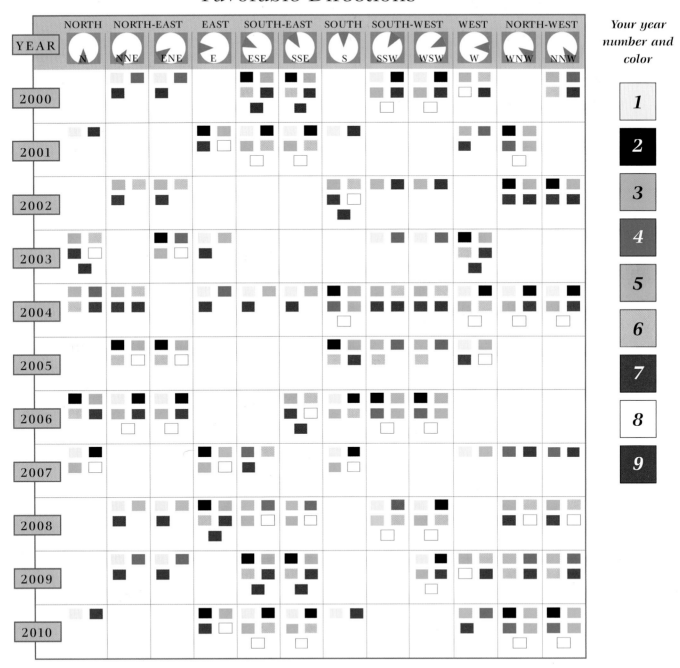

Mercury ☿

♈	Aries	♋	Cancer	♎	Libra	♑	Capricorn
♉	Taurus	♌	Leo	♏	Scorpio	♒	Aquarius
♊	Gemini	♍	Virgo	♐	Sagittarius	♓	Pisces

♒	18 1 2000	♎	31 8 2001	♊	12 6 2003	♐	4 11 2004
♓	5 2 2000	♏	7 11 2001	♋	29 6 2003	♑	9 1 2005
♈	12 4 2000	♐	26 11 2001	♌	13 7 2003	♒	29 1 2005
♉	29 4 2000	♑	15 12 2001	♍	30 7 2003	♓	16 2 2005
♊	14 5 2000	♒	3 1 2002	♌	6 10 2003	♈	5 3 2005
♋	30 5 2000	♑	4 2 2002	♏	24 10 2003	♉	12 5 2005
♌	6 8 2000	♒	13 2 2002	♐	12 11 2003	♊	28 5 2005
♍	22 8 2000	♓	11 3 2002	♑	2 12 2003	♋	11 6 2005
♎	7 9 2000	♈	29 3 2002	♐	30 12 2003	♌	28 6 2005
♏	28 9 2000	♉	13 4 2002	♑	14 1 2004	♍	4 9 2005
♎	7 11 2000	♊	30 4 2002	♒	6 2 2004	♎	20 9 2005
♏	7 11 2000	♋	7 7 2002	♓	25 2 2004	♏	8 10 2005
♐	3 12 2000	♌	21 7 2002	♈	12 3 2004	♐	30 10 2005
♑	22 12 2000	♍	6 8 2002	♉	1 4 2004	♏	26 11 2005
♒	10 1 2001	♎	26 8 2002	♈	12 4 2004	♐	12 12 2005
♓	6 2 2001	♍	3 10 2002	♉	15 5 2004	♑	3 1 2006
♒	6 2 2001	♎	10 10 2002	♊	5 6 2004	♒	22 1 2006
♓	16 3 2001	♏	31 10 2002	♋	19 6 2004	♓	8 2 2006
♈	6 4 2001	♐	19 11 2002	♌	4 7 2004	♈	16 4 2006
♉	21 4 2001	♑	8 12 2002	♍	25 7 2004	♉	5 5 2006
♊	6 5 2001	♒	12 2 2003	♌	24 8 2004	♊	19 5 2006
♋	12 7 2001	♓	4 3 2003	♍	9 9 2004	♋	3 6 2006
♌	30 7 2001	♈	21 3 2003	♎	28 9 2004	♌	29 6 2006
♍	14 8 2001	♉	5 4 2003	♏	15 10 2004	♋	9 7 2006

NB Dates are written day, month, and year

Mercury ☿ (continued)

♈	Aries	♋	Cancer	♎	Libra	♑	Capricorn
♉	Taurus	♌	Leo	♏	Scorpio	♒	Aquarius
♊	Gemini	♍	Virgo	♐	Sagittarius	♓	Pisces

Sign	Date	Sign	Date	Sign	Date	Sign	Date
♋	9 7 2006	♓	14 3 2008	♍	17 9 2009	♋	16 6 2011
♌	10 8 2006	♈	2 4 2008	♎	9 10 2009	♌	2 7 2011
♍	27 8 2006	♉	17 4 2008	♏	28 10 2009	♍	29 7 2011
♎	12 9 2006	♊	2 5 2008	♐	15 11 2009	♌	7 8 2011
♏	2 10 2006	♋	10 7 2008	♑	5 12 2009	♍	8 9 2011
♐	7 12 2006	♌	26 7 2008	♒	10 2 2010	♎	25 9 2011
♑	27 12 2006	♍	10 8 2008	♓	1 3 2010	♏	13 10 2011
♒	15 1 2007	♎	29 8 2008	♈	17 3 2010	♐	2 11 2011
♓	2 2 2007	♏	4 11 2008	♉	2 4 2010	♑	8 1 2012
♒	26 2 2007	♐	23 11 2008	♊	9 6 2010	♒	27 1 2012
♓	17 3 2007	♑	12 12 2008	♋	25 6 2010	♓	13 2 2012
♈	10 4 2007	♒	1 1 2009	♌	9 7 2010	♈	2 3 2012
♉	27 4 2007	♑	21 1 2009	♍	27 7 2010	♓	23 3 2012
♊	11 5 2007	♒	14 2 2009	♎	3 10 2010	♈	16 4 2012
♋	28 5 2007	♓	8 3 2009	♏	20 10 2010	♉	8 5 2012
♌	4 8 2007	♈	25 3 2009	♐	8 11 2010	♊	24 5 2012
♍	19 8 2007	♉	9 4 2009	♑	30 11 2010	♋	7 6 2012
♎	5 9 2007	♊	1 5 2009	♐	18 12 2010	♌	25 6 2012
♏	27 9 2007	♉	13 5 2009	♑	13 1 2011	♍	31 8 2012
♎	24 10 2007	♊	13 6 2009	♒	3 2 2011	♎	16 9 2012
♏	10 11 2007	♋	3 7 2009	♓	21 2 2011	♏	5 10 2012
♐	1 12 2007	♌	17 7 2009	♈	9 3 2011	♐	29 10 2012
♑	20 12 2007	♍	2 8 2009	♉	15 5 2011	♏	14 11 2012
♒	7 1 2008	♎	25 8 2009	♊	2 6 2011	♐	10 12 2012
						♑	31 12 2012

NB Dates are written day, month, and year

Astrological Tables

Venus ♀

♈	Aries	♋	Cancer	♎	Libra	♑	Capricorn
♉	Taurus	♌	Leo	♏	Scorpio	♒	Aquarius
♊	Gemini	♍	Virgo	♐	Sagittarius	♓	Pisces

♑	24 1 2000	♑	26 12 2001	♑	26 11 2003	♑	5 11 2005
♒	17 2 2000	♒	18 1 2002	♒	21 12 2003	♒	16 12 2005
♓	13 3 2000	♓	11 2 2002	♓	14 1 2004	♑	31 12 2005
♈	6 4 2000	♈	7 3 2002	♈	8 2 2004	♒	5 3 2006
♉	30 4 2000	♉	1 4 2002	♉	5 3 2004	♓	5 4 2006
♊	25 5 2000	♊	25 4 2002	♊	3 4 2004	♈	3 5 2006
♋	18 6 2000	♋	20 5 2002	♋	7 8 2004	♉	29 5 2006
♌	13 7 2000	♌	14 6 2002	♌	6 9 2004	♊	23 6 2006
♍	6 8 2000	♍	10 7 2002	♍	3 10 2004	♋	18 7 2006
♎	30 8 2000	♎	7 8 2002	♎	28 10 2004	♌	12 8 2006
♏	24 9 2000	♏	8 9 2002	♏	22 11 2004	♍	6 9 2006
♐	19 10 2000	♐	7 1 2003	♐	16 12 2004	♎	30 9 2006
♑	12 11 2000	♑	4 2 2003	♑	9 1 2005	♏	24 10 2006
♒	8 12 2000	♒	2 3 2003	♒	2 2 2005	♐	17 11 2006
♓	3 1 2001	♓	27 3 2003	♓	26 2 2005	♑	11 12 2006
♈	2 2 2001	♈	21 4 2003	♈	22 3 2005	♒	3 1 2007
♉	6 6 2001	♉	16 5 2003	♉	15 4 2005	♓	27 1 2007
♊	5 7 2001	♊	9 6 2003	♊	9 5 2005	♈	21 2 2007
♋	1 8 2001	♋	4 7 2003	♋	3 6 2005	♉	17 3 2007
♌	26 8 2001	♌	28 7 2003	♌	28 6 2005	♊	11 4 2007
♍	20 9 2001	♍	22 8 2003	♍	22 7 2005	♋	8 5 2007
♎	15 10 2001	♎	15 9 2003	♎	16 8 2005	♌	5 6 2007
♏	8 11 2001	♏	9 10 2003	♏	11 9 2005	♍	14 7 2007
♐	2 12 2001	♐	2 11 2003	♐	7 10 2005	♌	8 8 2007

NB Dates are written day, month, and year

Astrological Tables

Venus ♀ (continued)

♍	7	10	2007	♒	7	12	2008	♉	31	3	2010	♌	28	7	2011
♎	8	11	2007	♓	3	1	2009	♊	25	4	2010	♍	21	8	2011
♏	5	12	2007	♈	2	2	2009	♋	19	5	2010	♎	15	9	2011
♐	30	12	2007	♓	12	4	2009	♌	14	6	2010	♏	9	10	2011
♑	24	1	2008	♈	23	4	2009	♍	10	7	2010	♐	2	11	2011
♒	17	2	2008	♉	6	6	2009	♎	6	8	2010	♑	26	11	2011
♓	12	3	2008	♊	5	7	2009	♏	8	9	2010	♒	20	12	2011
♈	6	4	2008	♋	31	7	2009	♎	8	11	2010	♓	14	1	2012
♉	30	4	2008	♌	26	8	2009	♏	29	11	2010	♈	8	2	2012
♊	24	5	2008	♍	20	9	2009	♐	7	1	2011	♉	5	3	2012
♋	18	6	2008	♎	14	10	2009	♑	4	2	2011	♊	3	4	2012
♌	12	7	2008	♏	7	11	2009	♒	2	3	2011	♋	7	8	2012
♍	5	8	2008	♐	1	12	2009	♓	27	3	2011	♌	6	9	2012
♎	30	8	2008	♑	25	12	2009	♈	21	4	2011	♍	3	10	2012
♏	23	9	2008	♒	18	1	2010	♉	15	5	2011	♎	28	10	2012
♐	18	10	2008	♓	11	2	2010	♊	9	6	2011	♏	22	11	2012
♑	12	11	2008	♈	7	3	2010	♋	4	7	2011	♐	16	12	2012

Jupiter ♃

♈	23	10	1999	♍	27	8	2003	♒	5	1	2009	♉	4	6	2011
♉	14	2	2000	♎	25	9	2004	♓	18	1	2010	♊	11	6	2012
♊	30	6	2000	♏	26	10	2005	♈	6	6	2010				
♋	13	7	2001	♐	24	11	2006	♓	9	9	2010				
♌	1	8	2002	♑	18	12	2007	♈	22	1	2011				

Saturn Venus ♄

♉	1	3	1999	♊	20	4	2001	♍	2	9	2007	♎	21	7	2010
♊	10	8	2000	♋	4	6	2003	♎	29	10	2009	♏	5	10	2012
♉	15	10	2000	♌	16	7	2005	♍	7	4	2010				

Index

Acknowledgments

Carroll & Brown would like to thank:

Dawn Henderson for editorial assistance;

Karol Davies & Paul Stradling for production;

Rowena Feeny for desktop help;

Eric Biss for the ephemeris;

Hilary Bird for the index.

Illustration

Mark Preston: pages 16, 29, 43, 46–53, 70–71, 78–79, 84–85, 86, 91, 93, 97, 99, 105, 108–9, 136, 155, 158–9, 164, 170, 172–3. markp@mailbox.co.uk

Paul Canny: pages 18–21, 22–25, 66–69, 73–75, 80–82, 100–1, 118–22, 137, 139–56, 166–9. canny@talk21.com

Jules Selmes: pages 39, 55, 62, 83, 114, 127, 160

Russ Widstrand: pages 31, 59, 133. www.widstrand.com

Nanette Hoogslag: page 131

Bibliography

Most of the systems of divination in this book are from a body of ancient occult knowledge that is available in many forms and which was passed to me by the late Christine Hartley and other mentors. The following books have also been drawn upon:

The Zodiac Pack, Judy Hall (Findhorn Press, Inverness, 1996)

Napoleon's Book of Fate, Foulshams Home Library (Foulshams, London, 1958)

The Complete Illustrated Book of Divination and Prophecy, Walter B. Gibson and Litzka R. Gibson (Souvenir Press, London, 1974)

The Complete Book of the Occult and Fortune Telling, Introduction by M.C. Poinsot (Tudor Publishing Co., New York, 1939)

Divination: the search for meaning, Cherry Gilchrist (Dryad Press, London, 1987)

Spectrobiology, Maryla De Chrapowicki (C.W. Daniel, London, 1939)

Your Hand in Love, Bettina Luxon and Linda Dearsley (Rosters Ltd, London, 1989)

Medical Palmistry, Eugene Scheimann & Nathaniel Altman (Aquarian Press, Wellingborough, 1989)

Card Fortune Telling, Charles Thorpe (Foulsham, Cippenham, 1989)

Stress and the Sun Signs, Rupert J. Sewell (Aquarian Press, Wellingborough, 1981)

A Practical Guide to Geomantic Divination, Israel Regardie (Aquarian Press, London, 1972)

Self Mastery and Fate with the Cycles of Life, H. Spencer Lewis (Supreme Grand Lodge of AMORC, San Jose 1929)

Feng Shui Astrology, Simon Brown (Ward Lock, London, 1999)

Complete Guide to Nine Star Ki, Bob Sachs (Element, Shaftesbury, 1992)

The Book of Runes, Ralph Blum (Michael Joseph, London, 1984)

The Illustrated Guide to Astrology, Judy Hall (Godsfield Press, Alresford, 1998)

Chinese Astrology, Man-Ho Kwok (Charles E Tuttle Co. Inc, Boston, 1997)

The I Ching, Richard Wilhelm edition trans. Cary F. Baynes (Routledge & Kegan Paul, London, 1951)

I Ching, translated and edited by John Blofeld (Penguin Arkana, London, 1991)

The Life You Were Born to Live, Dan Millman (H J Kramer Inc Tiburon, 1993)